MALAWI WOMEN OF GOD

A PLAN ONLY GOD COULD DEVISE

MISTI STEVENS

Author's Tranquility Press
ATLANTA, GEORGIA

Misti Stevens /Author's Tranquility Press
3800 Camp Creek Pkwy SW Bldg. 1400-116 #1255
Atlanta, GA 30331, USA
www.authorstranquilitypress.com

Publisher's Note: This is non-fiction.

Ordering Information:
Quantity sales. Special discounts are available on quantity purchases by corporations, associations, and others. For details, contact the "Special Sales Department" at the address above.

MALAWI WOMEN OF GOD/Misti Stevens
Hardback: 978-1-961908-40-6
Paperback: 978-1-961908-41-3
eBook: 978-1-961908-42-0

Scripture quotations marked KJV are from the Holy Bible, King James Version (Authorized Version). First published in 1611. Quoted from the KJV Classic Reference Bible, Copyright © 1983 by The Zondervan Corporation

ACKNOWLEDGEMENTS

None of this would have happened if I did not have a husband who truly puts God first in his life. Wendell and I would like to thank all those who have allowed us to be the face of this mission work.

Members of the…

Malawi churches of Christ
Alston Road church of Christ
Nashua church of Christ
Prescott Valley church of Christ
Valley church of Christ

Special thanks go to all the sisters and brothers who have made teaching supplies, donated their time and money, and those who have prayed for our success, because that is from God, and Him alone. Finally, all the work we do in Malawi is possible because of three people, Larry Vinson, Shadreck Nyambo, and Lazarus Nguluwe you are our heroes.

All profits from this book are donated to the Malawi missionary work.

TABLE OF CONTENTS

INTRODUCTION

Who knew that a promise my husband and I made to each other while we were dating would lead to missionary work across the globe? Only God could devise the plan to send us to Malawi, a nation we had to look up on a map, whose language we did not speak, and to a culture so different from our own.

In 2018, we fulfilled our dream of visiting the Holy Land, with Barry Britnell on an Exploring Bible Lands tour. It was there that we met Brother Larry Vinson, a missionary working in Malawi. Larry and I peculiarly started our friendship, in Hezekiah's tunnel which was built to bring water into Jerusalem during a siege. Think dark, confining, and wet. Larry, who stands at 6'6", faced a challenge in this part of the tour. So, imagine, you are standing in

anywhere from 6 inches to 2 feet of water, the only light you have is from the flashlights of those in the tunnel, the floor is uneven, the ceiling sporadically falls to 5'6" and you do not have a flashlight of your own.

That was Larry, who stood directly behind me on the tour, did I say that the width of the tunnel was barely shoulder wide? Sympathy, and later empathy when I too had to bend down to walk, encouraged me to point my headlamp backward to light Larry's way. That was the start of the friendship between Larry, Wendell my husband, and I, one built on trust. One that God would use to send us across the globe.

But I get ahead of myself, at the end of the trip to Israel, we invited Larry to visit the church we attended in Missouri to tell people about his work in Malawi. His preaching, no-nonsense and biblically based, and description of people who were genuinely hungering and thirsting for righteousness (Matthew 5:6) led us to ask what we could do to help, *"Is there anything we can do?"* Boy, were we surprised when Larry answered, "Honestly, we need teachers," what a bombshell? We were expecting him to ask for Bibles or funding, not us. So, we had to decide, did we really mean "anything," considering how God tells us the seriousness of paying our vows to Him in *Ecclesiastes 4:4-6, "When thou vowest a vow unto God, defer not to pay it; for he hath no pleasure in fools: pay that which thou has vowed."*

We decided to go to Malawi, not knowing what it would cost, if we would be accepted, and whether it was really "safe." This study guide contains the lessons shared with the women over the five years that we made those trips. It also contains some of the lessons that I learned from the Christians in Malawi. There is no way we could adequately express the love, admiration, and thankfulness felt towards these, my sisters, and the inspiration they have been to me and others who have accompanied us to Malawi to teach and learn.

REFLECTION

At the beginning of this adventure two main questions kept popping into my mind. "What subject do you want me to teach and who will I be teaching?" I asked Larry those questions numerous times over the next ten months while we prepared to make our first trip to Malawi. From a teacher's standpoint, they didn't seem unreasonable but unknowingly I was learning one of the first lessons from our trip: have faith, God is working things out. We didn't know which villages we would teach in, what facilities we would have to teach in, or how long we would be asked to teach, and many more variables we hadn't even thought of. My husband often compares teaching in Malawi to teaching in America in the 1800s. Whereas my common questions were "will there be a Smartboard or at least a projector?" The questions became, "How do you communicate principles when you don't even know their culture?" I was about to face a reality that would teach me that God truly provides.

I became frustrated when Larry's answers continued to be, "Aww Miss Misti I know whatever you teach will be good." Questions were circling in my head so loudly I was surprised he could not hear them in Africa. "Excuse me, doesn't he know that I need to know what ages I will teach to know what level to prepare for?" I asked my husband, who was tasked with teaching the men, "How am I supposed to teach a class of children and women anything that would adapt and help both?" I was asking the wrong individual, I needed to get down on my knees and ask God. When I finally did, I made an interesting discovery. Cecil Leach was my grandfather, my spiritual mentor, and the wisest man I've known. He seldom spoke but when he did, people listened. My loss at his passing is still palatable today.

I decided to go through all the Bible class materials we had in our house. Quite an undertaking since it includes over 200 years of lessons taught by my grandparents, parents, aunts, myself, and my husband, you get the point. Amid the various Bibles, I found a handful of notes, verses, which were used with simple lesson titles, and the writing was my Grandpa's. I cried; God had given me the lessons I should teach by resurrecting Grandpa Leach's faithfulness in those small slips of paper. He had also provided me a tangible reminder of *Hebrews 12:1 "Wherefore seeing we also are compassed about with so great a cloud of witnesses, let us lay aside every weight, and the sin which doth so easily beset us, and let us run with patience the race that is set before us.* The next lesson was developed from those notes.

CHAPTER 1

THE SUPREMACY OF GOD'S WORD
Ukulu wa Mawu a Mulungu

2 Timothy 3:16-17 All scripture is given by inspiration of God, and is profitable for doctrine, for reproof, for correction, for instruction in righteousness, that the man of God may be complete, thoroughly equipped for every good work.

Inspired means, God breathed, while the Bible had many different writers there was only One author.

2 Peter 1:20-21 Knowing this first, that no prophecy of scripture is of any private interpretation, for prophecy never came by the will of man, but holy men of God spoke as they were moved by the Holy Spirit.

In other words, it doesn't matter what I say, or what any other teacher says or thinks if it is not backed up by the Bible, God's word, it is not a part of His will. God gave us the Bible for many good works, let's look at some of those.

DOCTRINE

1 Corinthians 16:1-2 Now concerning the collection of the saints, as I have given orders to the churches of Galatia, so you must do also. On the first day of the week let each one of you lay something aside, storing up as he may prosper, that there be no collections when I come.

Doctrine tells us what we as Christians and a church should do and gives us examples of how to do it. For example, we as

Christians need to humble ourselves before God and that is evident when we thank Him for the blessings we receive and help supply the needs of the saints through contributions made from the blessings He has given us.

REFROOF

The Bible is also a source of reproof, an expression of blame or disapproval. This helps us see the sin in our lives and become more like Christ. Here are some examples.

Galatians 2:11-14 But when Peter had come to Antioch, I withstood him to his face, because he was to be blamed.

Even though Jesus had given the keys of the kingdom, or church to Peter *(Matthew 16:19)* he was having a hard time standing up for God's plan to allow gentiles to enter the church. Paul saw this and knew Peter was wrong, so he reproved him in love using God's word.

CORRECTIONS

Paul used the word of God to correct misunderstandings and misapplication of God's word. He also tells us how we should do that in *Galatians 6:1,* in a spirit of gentleness with care in case we become wrong.

Acts 19:3-5 And he said unto them, "Into what then were you baptized?" So, they said, "Into John's baptism." Then Paul said, "John indeed baptized with the baptism of repentance, saying to the people that they should believe in Him who would come after him, that is, on Christ Jesus." When they heard this, they were baptized in the name of the Lord Jesus."

INSTRUCTION

There are many scriptures that teach us to train others and ourselves in the scriptures. Parents teach children, men teach publicly in the assembly and sisters have a special bond based on instruction.

Titus 2:3-5 The older women likewise that they be reverent in behavior, not slanderers not given to much wine, teachers of good things that they admonish the young women to love their husbands, to love their children, to be discreet, chaste, homemakers, good, obedient to their own husbands, that the word of God may not be blasphemed.

God told women to teach those who are younger than us. He tells us what to teach, and defines what He expects, in the Bible. For example in Titus we see that older women are to teach younger women to love, but what exactly does God mean when He says "love"? We know the answer to that question because God tells us in *I Corinthians 13:4-8.*

Love never fails, and is kind; love does not envy, love does not parade itself, is not puffed up; does not behave rudely, does not seek its own, is not provoked, thinks no evil; does not rejoice in iniquity; but rejoices in truth; bears all things, believes all things, hopes all things, endures all things. Love never fails…

We also teach the supremacy of God's word, when we use the Bible and stay true to its teachings. We do this by loving and respecting the truth as we see in *1 Thessalonians 2:10-12.*

And with all unrighteous deception among those who perish; because they did not receive the love of the truth, that they might be saved. And for this reason, God will send them a strong delusion, that they should behave a lie, that they all may be condemned who do not believe the truth but had pleasure in unrighteousness.

In order to love the truth we must know the truth. The people in Berea respected and loved the truth and that was demonstrated by their use of the truth.

Acts 17:11 These were more fair-minded than those in Thessalonica, in that they received the word with all readiness, and searched the scriptures daily to find out whether these things were so.

We need to study God's word to know what it says, with a desire and love for the truth.

REFLECTION

That first lesson taught me many things, one of them was that God trains us for what He knows He will use us for. My mental argument over my inability to teach adult women and with children in the same classroom quickly became a moot point. First, there were no classrooms, at least not to our standards. The picture of the gathering that you saw earlier was the building we first taught in. They were proud of that building and knew God had blessed them to have it as a place of worship. What a different perspective, there were no pews, carpet, or air conditioning, not even a roof. But they overwhelmingly appreciated that God had given them a foundation to build on.

Our lesson that day included a sermon, songs, separate classes for the men and women, and another sermon all of which lasted three hours, through which the women sat on concrete, behind the men, taking care of the children, while the sun beat down on their backs listening attentively because they understood they were hearing the words of life. They didn't know how to read, had no Bibles of their own but they were hungering and thirsting for righteousness in a way most never had. I was humbled.

God also taught me that what I saw as a problem He was going to use as an opening to teach. After the first sermon the women moved to the other "room" in the building. As we were gathering one of the babies began to cry. My grandmother's instincts kicked in and my face transformed to that "Oh, it's okay, sweetie," look that we have all seen. I asked, tentatively, because it was my first interaction with the mothers if I could hold the child. The mother looked like she had seen a ghost and frankly had the child stopped crying for anyone else I would have been the last person she gave the child to. Traditional Shaman's in Malawi teach that white people will steal one's soul and not only was my skin white so was my hair. After an elderly woman "suggested" she let me hold the child, she passed her to me. That is faith! Then God worked His wonders, I started comforting the child, and she was calmed. All the eyes of the women who had come to see this stranger talk about God now felt a bond with me and I with them. So much so, that when the child started to cry again during the second sermon, about two hours later, the mother passed the baby back to me. In Dedza I am known as the baby comforter because God used what He I thought was a hindrance to open a door for the gospel.

CHAPTER 2

BEATITUDES: KINGDOM CITIZENS AND THEIR CHARACTER
Zosangalatsa Nzika za Ufumu ndi Makhalidwe Awo

REFLECTION

This lesson and the women there taught me once again to trust God. I was told when we entered the congregation that there would only be a sermon, no classes. But at the end of the lesson when we were getting into the truck there was a minor tumult. Soon, Shadreck, our interpreter came to us and explained that the women wanted to hear a lesson from me. "Help" was my first thought. I had only brought one lesson with me that morning, the one had taught at the previous congregation. The one that fifteen of the women had already heard. Now I was being asked to teach another lesson, granted I was given 5 minutes to gather my thoughts, and even though Shad said I could teach the same lesson again I cringed at the thought of wasting an opportunity for those who had come with us. After a deep breath I thought, "What do I know well enough that I could teach a Bible lesson from the notes I have in my Bible?"

There are those who do not take notes in their Bibles, and I am not here to debate whether that should be done but consider this. In my Bible, I have notes from many family studies. That afternoon I turned to the Beatitudes and taught a lesson I had been taught; God had prepared me, I only had to have faith to get out of my own way. Many of us have a wealth of training that has prepared us to reach so many, only we refuse to use it because of what might be asked, or how people might respond. Jesus addresses this action in the parable of the talents, are we going to be the workers that come back and present Jesus with the earnings of our labor, or are we the servant who cowers from fear and is punished because we never used the talents God gave us? *Matthew 25:14-30*

We are here because we believe in God and are willing to study His word to learn how to enter His kingdom. There is a door we must enter to be part of His kingdom. We read about that door in John.

John 10:7 Then said Jesus unto them again, Verily, verily, I say unto you, I am the door of the sheep. All that ever came before me are thieves and robbers: but the sheep did not hear them. I am the door: by Me if any man enters, he shall be saved, and shall go in and out, and find pasture.

Jesus is the door to the kingdom of God. If we want to be a member of God's kingdom and eventually go to heaven, we must walk in Jesus' teaching and develop the character God wants us to have. God tells us how we do that in *Matt 5:1-10*. The first step in having the character of a kingdom citizen.

Matthew 5:3 Blessed are the poor in spirit, for theirs is the kingdom of heaven.

How do we become poor in Spirit?

Romans 5:8 But God commandeth His love toward us, in that, while we were yet sinners, Christ died for us. Much more then, being now justified by His blood, we shall be saved from wrath through Him. For if, when we were enemies, we were reconciled to God by the death of His Son, much more, being reconciled, we all be saved by His life.

They put nails through the hands and feet of Jesus, spat on Him, shredded His back with a whip and all when completely innocent. Would we pay that cost? When we recognize what God paid for us to be His we become poor in spirit, then we mourn.

Matthew 5:4 Blessed are those who mourn, for they shall be comforted.

Understanding the cost of our sins makes us mourn the cost that Jesus had to pay for us. The parable of the prodigal son helps us understand this principle.

Luke 15:18-22 I will arise and go to my father, and will say unto him, Father, I have sinned against heaven, and before thee, and am no more worthy to be called thy son, make me as one of thy hired servants. And he arose, and came to his father, But when he was yet a great way off, his father saw him, and had compassion, and ran, and fell on his neck and kissed him.

So, God not only gave His Son Jesus to pay the price for our sins, a price also we could not pay. When we mourn the fact that we put Jesus on the cross, He will comfort us. Our recognition that God was willing to pay such a significant cost to save us makes us meek.

Matthew 5:5 Blessed are the meek, for they shall inherit the earth.

The word 'meek' means 'gentle'. Jesus says that He is gentle.

Matthew 11:29 Take My yoke upon you and learn of Me; for I am meek and lowly in heart: and ye shall find rest unto your souls.

When we remember and realize how kind God has been to us, we stop demanding what we think we deserve. We change our focus from self to others. Then God showers us with blessings.

Psalm 3:3 & 8 But Thou on Lord are a shield for me; my glory and the lifter of my head…Salvation belongeth to the Lord; Thy blessing is upon Thy people.

Malachi 3:10 Bring ye all the tithes into the storehouse, and there shall be food in My house, and prove Me. Now herewith, saith the Lord of hosts, if I will not open you the windows of heaven, and pour out a blessing, that there shall not be room enough to receive it.

When we realize the cost of our sins, we become poor in spirit and then we mourn, which makes us meek or gentle because we see how much we owe Him. When we do that, He showers us with even more blessings. How great is our God!

So, as we go toward the door of God's heavenly kingdom, we become poor in spirit, which leads us to mourn, we become meek when we recognize every good gift is from God which makes us hunger and thirst for His righteousness.

Matthew 5:6 Blessed are those who hunger and thirst for righteousness, for they shall be filled.

The more we recognize how much we need God, the more we crave His word.

Isaiah 55:1-3 Ho! Everyone who thirsts, come to the waters; and you who have no money, come, and buy and eat. Yes, come, buy, and eat. Yes, come buy wine and milk without price. Why do you spend money for what is not bread and your wages for what does not satisfy? Listen diligently to me and eat what is good; and let your soul delight itself in abundance. Incline your ear and come to Me. Hear and your soul shall live; and I will make an everlasting covenant with you.

So many times, we crave what the world offers us. But when we are poor in spirit, mourn for the cost of our sin, and become meek, understanding we are nothing without God, we will crave the life-giving words of God, and He has promised that we will be filled. Then as God has been merciful to us, we will become merciful to others.

Matthew 5:7 Blessed are the merciful, for they shall obtain mercy.

King David writes of God's mercy in *Psalm 145:9 The Lord is good to all, and His tender mercies are over all His works. Jesus tells us we cannot expect mercy if we will not show mercy.*

Matthew 6:12 And forgive us our debts, as we forgive our debtors.

God warns us what to expect if we will not forgive our sisters and brothers in Christ.

Matthew 18:33-35 Should you not also have had compassion on your fellow servants, just as I pitied you? And his master was angry, and delivered him to the torturers until he should pay all that was due him. "So my Father in heaven will also do to each of you if you, from his heart do not forgive his brother his trespasses."

So, we have a choice, we can forgive others when they ask for forgiveness, or we can lose our forgiveness from God and be held accountable for the immense debt we owe God. Once we receive mercy, God expects us to strive to keep our hearts pure.

Matthew 5:8 Blessed are the pure in heart, for they shall see God.

In the Psalms, God explains how being poor in spirit encourages us to maintain a pure heart.

Psalm 24:4-5 He who has clean hands and a pure heart, who has not lifted his soul to an idol, nor sworn deceitfully. He shall bless from the Lord (YHWH) and righteousness from the God (Elohe) of our salvation.

When we are pure in heart God uses us as peacemakers.

Matthew 5:9 Blessed are the peacemakers, for they shall be called sons of God.

When we share these truths, we help others have peace with God; we are peacemakers.

Romans 10:15 How beautiful are the feet of those who preach the gospel of peace, who bring glad tidings of good things.

Jesus talks about this peace in *John 14:27* and *Colossians 3:15*.

Peace I leave with you, my peace I give to you, not as the world gives do I give to you. Let not your heart be troubled, neither let it be afraid. The only peace that is true is through Christ and God.

And let the peace of God rule in your hearts, to which also you were called in one body, and be thankful.

We have God's peace and can become peacemakers when we are pure in heart.

2 Timothy 2:22 Flee also youthful lusts; but pursue righteousness, faith, love, peace with those who call on the Lord our of a pure heart.

Our peace is in Christ and the devil will try to make us give up on that hope and peace but Jesus says in Matthew 5:10-12…

Blessed are those who are persecuted for righteousness' sake, for theirs is the kingdom of heaven. Blessed are you when they revile and persecute you, and say all kinds of evil against you falsely for My sake. Rejoice and be exceedingly glad, for great is your reward before you.

Let's live a life worthy of our Father's reward.

REFLECTION

One of the incredible blessings of worshiping is singing. Members of Malawi congregations are not singing to prove they can carry a tune or worried about who will hear, they are singing to God. You can hear the praise in their hearts with each word. In 1981, I went to a lectureship with my father at Florida College. There were hundreds of us packed into a basketball gym singing praises to our King, led by R J Stevens. My dad, who had a booming bass voice that was lauded by many, stopped singing in the middle of one of the songs, On *Zion's Glorious Summit*. I looked over to see one of the last people in the world you would ever see cry wiping tears from his eyes, "This is what heaven will sound like." That is what Malawi sounded like, without the acoustics of a gymnasium the songs rang out through the surrounding villages giving God praise even from the back of a truck.

This stop on the trip was not planned. We were at the Kajuni Village congregation when the men asked if we would be willing to go to a small congregation that had recently started, not far away. The women you saw in the truck asked when we were leaving to go there if they could come with us. "Of course!" Fifteen women and one man climbed into the back of a Ford Ranger and started singing hymns, not stopping until we arrived at the next church. Would we be so willing to spend extra time worshiping God?

In this next place as well as others crowds often overflowed the buildings and we moved outside in God's creation and worshiped without murmuring Him who created all that they saw.

CHAPTER 3

THE BEAUTY OF HOLINESS
Kukongola kwa Chiyero

The beauty of God's holiness is seen in all of God's creation. That beauty should inspire respect and reverence for God. When we respect and revere God the way we should we are bringing an offering to Him. Instead of coming empty handed we are giving Him the gift, our thankfulness and respect.

I Chronicles 16:29 Give to the Lord, the glory due His name; Bring an offering, and come before Him. Oh, worship the Lord in the beauty of holiness!

II Chronicles 20:21 And when he had consulted with the people, he appointed those who should sing to the Lord, and who should praise the beauty of holiness, as they went out before the army and were saying: "Praise the Lord, For His mercy endures forever."

When we come to God with an offering, He is merciful to us. Our offering is ourselves. We owe respect and praise to God.

Psalm 29:2 Give unto the Lord the glory due to His name; Worship the Lord in the beauty of holiness.

Psalm 96:9 Oh, worship the Lord in the beauty of holiness! Tremble before Him, all the earth.

When we witness the beauty of God's creation and plan for our salvation it inspires respect, humility, and a desire to worship Him because of His holiness. Our greatest offering is of ourselves; to His glory.

Psalm 110:3 Your people shall be volunteers in the day of Your power; In the beauties of holiness, from the womb of the morning, You have the dew of Your youth.

We owe God our lives from our earliest days. And the beauty of that is when we give ourselves to Him, we are lovely to God. The loveliest person is the one whose life most nearly conforms to God's teachings and whose feet walk closest in the steps of the perfect pattern. The Bible refers to this as godliness, righteousness, or holiness. Part of that beauty is seen in the reflection of the radiance of heaven. When Jesus came to this world, He was the light of the world.

John 9:5 As long as I am in the world, I am the light of the world.

Without that light, without Him, we all stumble. Today, Christ's disciples are the light of the world.

Matthew 5:14-16 You are the light of the world. A city that is set on a hill cannot be hidden. Nor do they light a lamp and put it under a basket, but on a lampstand, and it gives light to all who are in the house. Let your light so shine before men, that they may see your good works and glorify your Father in heaven.

When we live holy lives the world sees the loveliness of God because His light shines in us. But how do we do this? First, we must deliberately learn His word. And apply it to our lives. Improvement begins with self-examination.

Romans 2:13 For not the hearers of the law are just in the sight of God, but the doers of the law will be justified.

Psalms 119:59 I thought about my ways and turned my feet to Your testimonies.

God's word furnishes the mirror for our soul and is the only guide for spiritual improvement.

James 1:22-25 But be doers of the word, and not hearers only, deceiving yourselves. For if anyone is a hearer of the word and not a doer, he is like a man observing his natural face in a mirror; for he observes himself, goes away, and immediately forgets what king of man he was. But he who looks into the perfect law of liberty and continues in it, and is not a forgetful hearer but a doer of the work, this one will be blessed in what he does.

If we choose to not use God's word, we will die and be judged for our sins that were never washed away. That judgment will be an eternal life in hell ff after we hear God's word, we ignore what God says. We must do His will that is why we are admonished to diligently study to show ourselves approved. So we can follow the example of the righteous one in Psalms 1.

2 Tim 2:15 Be diligent to present yourself approved to God, a worker who does not need to be ashamed, rightly dividing the word of truth.

Psalms 1:1-3 Blessed is the man who walks not in the counsel of the ungodly, nor stands in the path of sinners, nor sits in the seat of the scornful, but his delight is in the law of the Lord. And in His law, he meditates day and night. He shall be like a tree planted by the rivers of water, that brings forth its fruit in its season, whose leaf also shall not wither; and whatever he does shall prosper.

Notice we are to be a tree planted – a deliberate thing. That allows us to bring forth fruit – a blessing to others which will make us like a leaf that does not wither – a lovely evergreen. And the we shall prosper – have a future that is bright.

The loveliness that we have when we respect God, worship Him, and sacrifice our lives by committing to learn and follow His Word will never fade or die. But though our outward man perishes, yet the inward man is renewed day by day.

Isaiah 40:29-31 He gives power to the weak, and to those who have no might He increases strength. Even the youths shall faint and be weary, and the young men shall utterly fail, but those who wait on the Lord, shall renew their strength; they shall mount up with wings like eagles, they shall run and not be weary, they shall walk and not faint.

The beauty that is endurance is gained when we fear or respect the Lord. Obedience with God's law also makes a source of strength for others.

Proverbs 31:30 Charm is deceitful and beauty is vain, but a woman who fears the Lord, she shall be praised.

One of our heroes is Ella, a teenager who travelled the globe to teach others.

Proverbs 31:25-26 Strength and honor are her clothing; she shall rejoice in time to come. She opens her mouth with wisdom, and on her tongue is the law of kindness.

We have all been created with an outward woman that perishes and an inward woman that is renewed through service to God. According to God, the heart, the inward woman is what is important.

II Corinthians 4:16 Therefore, we do not lose heart. Even though our outward man is perishing, yet the inward man is being renewed day by day.

I Samuel 16:7 But the Lord said to Samuel, "Do not look at his appearance or at the height of his stature, because I have refused him. For the Lord does not see as man sees; for man looks at the outward appearance, but the Lord looks at the heart."

God uses both our outward and inner woman to fulfill His plans. The Lord described and used the physical appearance of many in the Bible to further His plans. Sarah and Esther are two examples.

Genesis 12:14-16 So it was, when Abram came into Egypt, that the Egyptians saw the woman, that she was very beautiful. The princes of Pharaoh also saw her and commended her to Pharaoh. And the woman was taken to Pharaoh's house. He treated Abram well for her sake…

Esther 2:7 and 16 And Mardecai had brought up Hadassah, that is Esther, his uncle's daughter, for she had neither father nor mother. The young woman was lovely and beautiful. When her father and mother died, Mordecai took her as his own daughter…The king loved Esther more than all the other women, and she obtained grace and favor in his sight more than all the virgins; so he set the royal crown upon her head and made her queen instead of Vashti.

Esther's plea saved the people of Israel.

Esther 8:6 For how can I endure to see the evil that will come to my people? Or how can I endure tosee the destruction of my kindred?

Respect for God is seen in every facet of our lives. Knowing this, what we wear should always glorify God.

1 Timothy 2:9, 10. In like manner also, that the women adorn themselves in modest apparel, with propriety and moderation, not with braided hair or gold or pearls or costly clothing, but which is proper for women professing godliness, with good works.

We must go to God's word to see how we should live and then live that way. There are evident traits in our lives if we do this.

James 1:25 But he who looks into the perfect law of liberty and continues in it, and is not a forgetful hearer but a doer of the work, this one will be blessed in what he does.

Colossians 3:12 Therefore, as the elect of God, holy and beloved, put on, tender mercies, kindness, humbleness of mind, meekness, long-suffering.

God wants us to recognize the consequences of failing to recognize, repent, and correct our spiritual imperfections.

James 1:22 But be doers of the word, and not hearers only, deceiving yourselves.

James 4:17 Therefore, to him who knows good and does not do it to him it is sin.

James 1:15 Then, when desire has conceived, it gives birth to sin; and sin, when it is full-grown, brings forth death.

Romans 6:23 For the wages of sin is death, but the gift of God is eternal life in Christ Jesus our Lord.

We need to accept Jesus' gift like the Jews in *Acts 2:36-47*, repent, and be baptized to wash away the sins that stain our spiritual body. It is only then that the loveliness of God will dwell in us.

Children seeking God.

REFLECTION

Learning from the children was a common occurrence in Malawi. One of those lessons came in the middle of the women trying to learn in a small classroom. While discipline may be dead in America it is still a part of the culture in Malawi. That was evident when the children from the congregation started gathering around the doors and windows of the borrowed classroom where we were studying. I admit that their efforts to see what was happening and hear what was being taught were distracting but they soon taught us all a lesson. The second time that one of the older women reprimanded them I did not need an interpreter to understand the gist of her message and her movement toward the door sent the youth scattering. But when a small group of brave, or some would have called them foolish, the children quickly returned and one of the youths called out, "You say you want us to learn but you keep us out."

Ouch, in *Matthew 19:14* Jesus reprimands the apostles for keeping the children from Him. When we read that scripture, we can sometimes sanctimoniously think, "I would never do that." But do our actions send that same message to the children seeking out a Holy God?

Hungering and thirsting for righteousness.

CHAPTER 4

TRAITS GOD HATES
Makhalidwe Amene Mulungu Amadana Nawo

Loving our spiritual family means ridding ourselves of traits that harm ourselves and others. That was the basis of this lesson.

II Timothy 3:1-3 But understand this: in the last days terrible times will come. For men will be lovers of themselves, lovers of money, boastful, arrogant, abusive, disobedient to their parents, ungrateful, unholy, unloving, unforgiving, slanderous, without self-control, brutal, without love of good, traitorous, reckless, conceited, lovers of pleasure rather than lovers of God.

1. Ungrateful like Eve, God gave her the perfect home, food, beautiful garden, and a husband who loved her and her actions said that they were not good enough.

Genesis 2:8-10, 16-17, 23-24 And the Lord God planted a garden eastward in Eden; and there he put the man whom he had formed. And out of the ground made the Lord God to grow every tree that is pleasant to the sight, and good for food; the tree of life also in the midst of the garden, and the tree of knowledge of good and evil. And a river went out of Eden to water the garden...And the Lord God commanded the man, saying, Of every tree of the garden thou mayest feely eat: But of the tree of the knowledge of good and evil, thou shalt not eat of it: for in the day that thou eatest thereof thou shalt surely die...And the rib, which the Lord God had taken from man, made he a woman, and brought her unto the man. And Adam said, This is now bone of my bones, and flesh of my flesh; she shall be called Woman, because she was taken out of Man. Therefore shall a man leave his father and his mother, and shall cleave unto his wife; and they shall be of one flesh.

Genesis 3:3-6 But of the fruit of the tree which is in the midst of the garden, God hath said, Ye shall not eat of it, neither shall ye touch it, lest ye die. And the serpent said unto the woman, Ye shall not surely die; For God doth know that in the day ye eat thereof, then your eyes shall be opened, and ye shall be as gods, knowing good and evil. And when the woman saw that the tree was good for food and that it was pleasant to the eyes, and a tree to be desired to make one wise, she took of the fruit thereof, and did eat, and gave also unto her husband with her, and he did eat.

2. Pride

Mark 7:21-22 For from within, out of the heart of men, proceed evil thoughts, adulteries, fornications, murders, thefts covetousness, wickedness, deceit, lasciviousness, an evil eye, blasphemy, pride, foolishness: All these evil things come from within, and defile the man.

3. Stubbornness

Deuteronomy 21:18-21 "If a man has a stubborn and rebellious son who will not obey the voice of his father or the voice of his mother, and, though they discipline him, will not listen to them, then his father and his mother shall take hold of him and bring him out to the elders of his city at the gate of the place where he lives, and they shall say to the elders of his city, 'This our son is stubborn and rebellious; he will not obey our voice; he is a glutton and a drunkard.' Then all the men of the city shall stone him to death with stones. So you shall purge the evil from your midst, and all Israel shall hear, and fear.

4. Envy

It was the sin of envy that drove the Jewish leaders to seek the death of Jesus.

Matthew 27:17-18 Pilate said unto them, Whom will ye that I release unto Barabbas, or Jesus which is called Christ? For he knew that for envy they had delivered Him.

Galatians 5:21 Envyings, murders, drunkenness, revelings, and such like: of the which I tell you before, as I have also told you in time past, that they which do such things shall not inherit the kingdom of God.

5. Anger

Romans 12:19 Dearly beloved, avenge not yourselves, but rather give place unto wrath: for it is written, Vengeance is mine; I will repay, saith the Lord.

6. Slander or Speak Evil against a Brother

James 3:8 Brothers, do not slander one another. Anyone who speaks against his brother or judges him speaks against the law and judges it. And if you judge the law, you are not a practitioner of the law, but a judge of it.

Proverbs 10:18 Whoever conceals hatred with lying lips and spreads slander is a fool.

7. Gossip

Ephesians 4:29 Do not let any unwholesome talk come out of your mouths, but only what is helpful for building others up according to their needs, that it may benefit those who listen.

Matthew 5:11 Blessed are you when people insult you, persecute you and falsely say all kinds of evil against you because of me.

8. Arrogance

Romans 12:16 Be of the same mind toward one another; do not be haughty in mind, but associate with the lowly. Do not be wise in your own estimation.

James 4:16 But as it is, you boast in your arrogance; all such boasting is evil.

CHAPTER 5

PICTURE OF A LOVELY LIFE
Chithunzi cha Moyo Wokandedwa

REFLECTION

If we look closely at this picture, we notice a termite hill that was nearly six feet tall. It was at the edge of the tarp where we sat worshiping. Not in the picture was the dog, goat, and chicken with her brood of chicks that passed through the congregation as we worshiped their maker. We also miss the ants that were so thick Shad, our interpreter, and my husband were sprayed with pesticide during the lesson. Loveliness can be seen in the willingness to sit on a concrete, or dirt floor for hours in a space where you are in constant contact with other people and animals, and the only restroom available is a hole surrounded by brush with no roof. Loveliness is a group that just met you asking you to feed their babies to demonstrate you are truly a part of their family.

Christ is the central figure of all time. The very foundations of the world were shaken and the course of civilization was changed by the solitary life of the Son of God. In the Bible God has given us four perspectives of Jesus. Matthew pictured for the Jews a King and His kingdom. Mark pictured the wonder working Man of Action. Luke portrayed the Ideal Man for the Greeks, who so admired manhood. John pictured God's Son, the embodiment of the Father, the Universal Savior. Jesus exemplifies the lovely life we all should have.

To Behold the Beauty of the Lord

Psalm 27:4 One thing have I desired ...to behold the beauty of the Lord.

1. Mankind have always longed to see God. Those of Old Testament times had God's word, but they had never seen Him. One reason Christ came into the world was to show us the Father. Beholding that loveliness enshrined in the life of Jesus of Nazareth gives us a picture of the Father.

John 14:9 Jesus saith unto him, "Have I been so long time with you, and yet hast thou not known me, Philip? He that hath seen Me hath seen the Father; and how sayest thou then, Shew us the Father?

2. The life of Christ bears testimony that true loveliness can be achieved regardless of physical characteristics. Though we have no description of Jesus' physical traits, Isaiah indicates that He was not handsome, yet His real beauty has never been equaled.

Isaiah 53:2 For He shall grow up before Him as a tender plant, and as a root out of a dry ground: He hath no form nor comeliness; and when we shall see Him, there is no beauty that we should desire Him.

Obedience and Respect for Authority

1. Jesus came into the world to save sinners. All other activities were incidental as His life was centered around this one glorious goal. This gave him spiritual poise, the ability to meet every blow of life unwaveringly and triumphantly. Nothing made Him lose His spiritual balance, which is important for us as well.

2 Timothy 2:15 Study to shew thyself approved unto God, a workman that needeth not to be ashamed, rightly dividing the word of truth.

2. The abundant life which Christ came to bring His followers cannot be achieved by aimless drifting and a life consumed by smaller things.

John 10:10 The thief cometh not, but for to steal, and to kill, and to destroy: I am come that they might have life, and that they might have it more abundantly.

Neither can it be achieved if our lives are centered on the wrong goal.

Ecclesiastes 12:13 Let us hear the conclusion of the whole matter: Fear God and keep His commandments for this is the whole duty of man.

This is the right goal for our life and the recipe for abundant living. Since we have only one life, we must appraise our present goals and consider the ends of all our labors.

Obedience and Respect for Authority

1. Jesus was obedient to His parents.

Luke 2:51 And He went down with them, and came to Nazareth, and was subject unto them: but His mother kept all these sayings in her heart.

A failure to learn obedience to authority is carried into every realm of life – obedience to school authorities, civil laws, elders, husband, employer, and God.

Philippians 2:7-8 But made Himself of no reputation, and took upon Him the form of a servant, and was made in the likeness of men: And being found in fashion as a man, He humbled Himself, and became obedient unto death, even the death of the cross.

Hebrews 10:8-9 Lo, I come to do Thy will, O God. He taketh away the first, that he may establish the second.

Christ's obedience and subject to the authority of the Father can be seen throughout his whole life. He kept God's law and taught others the necessity of doing so.

Hebrews 5:8-9 Though He were a Son, yet learned He obedience by the things which He suffered; And being made perfect, He became the author of eternal salvation unto all them that obey Him.

Firmness and Conviction

1. Loving and tender, yet the Son of God is also called the Lion of Judah.

Revelation 5:5 And one of the elders saith unto me, Weep not: behold, the Lion of the tribe of Juda, the Root of David, hath prevailed to open the book, and to loose the seven seals thereof.

And as such, when divine truth was challenged He taught that truth is fixed and unchangeable and that obedience to it is an absolute necessity.

John 8:24 I said therefore unto you, that ye shall die in your sins; for if ye believe not that I am He, ye shall die in your sins.

John 14:6 I am the way

Tenderness and Compassion

1. Only weak characters are cruel. Our Lord was strong enough to be tender. This was shown by His feeling for children *Luke 18:15-17.*

And they brought unto His also infants, that He would touch them: but when His disciples saw it, they rebuked them. But Jesus called them unto Him and said, Suffer little children to come unto Me, and forbid them not; for of such is the kingdom of God.

He also showed this with His love for the sinful and outcast.

Luke 7:36-50 And one of the Pharisees desire Him that He would eat with him. And He went into the Pharisee's house, and sat down to meat. And, behold, a woman in the city, which was a sinner, when she knew that Jesus sat at meat in the Pharisee's house, brought an alabaster box of ointment, And stood at his feet behind Him weeping, and began to wash His feet with tears, and did wipe them with the hairs of her head and kissed His feet, and anointed them with ointment. Now when the Pharisee which had beholden Him saw it, he spoke within himself, saying, This man, if He were a prophet, would have known who and what manner of woman this is that toucheth Him for she is a sinner. And Jesus answering said unto him, Simon, I have somewhat to say unto thee. And he saith Master, say on. There was a certain creditor which had two debtors: the one owed five hundred pence, and the other fifty. And when they had nothing to pay, he frankly forgave them both. Tell me therefore, which of them will love Him most? Simon answered and said, I suppose that he, to whom he forgave most. And He said unto Him, Thou has rightly judged. And He turned to the woman and said unto Simon, Seest though this woman? I entered into thine house, thou gavest me no water for My feet; but she hath washed My feet with tears, and wiped them with the hairs of her head. Thou gavest me no kiss, but the woman since the time I came in hath not ceased to kiss my feet. My head with oil thou didst not anoint: but this woman has anointed my feet with ointment. Wherefore I say unto thee,

Her sins, which are many, are forgiven; for she loved much; but to whom little if forgiven, the same loveth little. And He said unto her, "Thy sins are forgiven." And they that sat at meat with Him began to say within themselves, Who is this that forgiveth sins also: And He said to the woman, Thy faith hath saved thee; go in peace.

Jesus sympathized with the sorrowing. His heart yearned to help even those who rejected Him.

Luke 13:34 O Jerusalem, Jerusalem which killest the prophets, and stonest them that are sent unto thee; how often would I have gathered thy children together, as a hen doth gather her brood under her wings, and ye would not!

Jesus had the courage to care.

Jesus is the truth, and the life: no man cometh unto the Father, but by Me and He says…

Luke 13:3 I tell you, Nay: but, except ye repent, ye shall all likewise perish.

Matthew 7:14 Because straight is the gate, and narrow is the way, which leadeth unto life, and few there be that find it.

2. If we are to follow the lovely pattern, we must have strength enough to stand for the truths of God. No amount of pressure or temptation ever led Jesus to compromise the truth.

John 17:17-23 Sanctify them through Thy truth; Thy word is truth. As Thou hast sent me into the world, even so have I also sent them into the world. And for their sakes I sanctify myself, that they also might be sanctified through the truth. Neither pray I for these alone, but for them also which shall believe on me through their word; that they all may be one; as Thou, Father, are in Me, and I in Thee, that they also may be one is Us; that the world may believe that Thou hast sent me. And the glory which Thou gavest Me I have given them; that they may be one, even as

We are one: I in them, and Thou in Me, that they may be made perfect in one; and that the world may know that Thou hast sent me, and hast loved them, as Thou hast loved Me.

A Man of Sorrows Who Spread Joy to Others

Though physical strength me be measured by how much we can carry, spiritual strength is sometimes measured by how much we can bear. Christ is a heroic example for us all. The most sublime joys can be experienced only by those who have borne the weightiest griefs.

Philippians 4:4-7, 12-13 Rejoice in the Lord always: and again I say, Rejoice. Let your moderation be known unto all men. The Lord is at hand. Be careful for nothing; but in every thing by prayer and supplication with thanksgiving let your requests be made known unto God. And the peace of God, which passeth all understanding, shall keep your hearts and minds through Christ Jesus... I know both how to be abased, and I know how to abound; everywhere and in all things I am instructed both to be full and to be hungry, both to abound and to suffer need. I can do all things through Christ which strengthened me.

Close Communion with the Father

1.   *Revelation 1:8 I am Alpha and Omega.*

The first and last letters in the Greek alphabet. In other words: I am everything. There is nothing in all God's planning that is not centered in Christ. Man has no spiritual need or long which cannot be fulfilled by Christ. Man needs no example which is not furnished by Christ.

2. He suffered for us, leaving us an example, that we should follow His steps.

1 Peter 2:21-22 For even herunto were ye called; because Christ also suffered for us, leaving us an example, that ye should follow His steps: Who did no sin, neither was guile found in His mouth.

How God anointed Jesus of Nazareth with the Holy Ghost and with power; who went about doing good, and healing all that were oppressed of the devil; for God was with Him.

Nothing is more admirable than following Him.

2 Corinthians 12:9-10 And He said unto me, My grace is sufficient for thee; for My strength is made perfect in weakness. Most gladly therefore will I rather glory in my infirmities, that the power of Christ may rest upon me. Therefore I take pleasure in infirmities, in reproaches, in necessities, persecutions, in distresses for Christ's sake: for when I am weak, then am I strong.

3. "For in Him dwelleth all the fulness of the Godhead bodily," Colossians 2:9. Christ is the Lamb of God (John 1:29), the Bright and Morning Star (Revelation 22:16), the Bread of Life (Matthew 6:11), the Good Shepherd (John10:11). He is the Way, the Truth, and the Life (John 14:6). He is the Living Water (John 7:37-38) ; and after we take our little vessels to the ever-flowing stream and fill them to capacity, the source is still inexhaustible (Revelation 22:17). He is the Light of the World (John 8:12), the Resurrection and the Life (John 11:25). Only through Christ is there salvation for the sinful and rest for the weary (Matthew 11:28).

And he says,

Behold I stand at the door, and knock; if any man heareth my voice, and open the door. I will come into him, and will sup with him, and He with me. Revelation 3:20

PRAISE GOD!

CHAPTER 6

JOY THROUGH RIGHTEOUSNESS
Chimwemwe kudzera mu Chilungamo

John 15:9-11 As the Father loved Me, I have also loved you; abide in My love. If you keep my commandments, you will abide in My love; just as I have kept My Father's commandments and bide in His love. These things I have spoken to you, that My joy may remain in you, and that your joy may be full.

Obtaining joy is a bi-product of doing God's will.

In the parable of the talents, we see that when we faithfully use the skills God gives us, He brings us into His joy.

Matthew 25:14-15 For the kingdom of heaven is like a man traveling to a far country, who called his own servants and delivered his goods to them. And to one he gave five talents, to another two, and to another one, to each according to his own ability, and immediately he went on a journey.

God has given each of us talents, things we do well. While we are here we are supposed to identify and use our talents, or gifts, to help His kingdom grow.

Matthew 25:19-21 After a long time, the lord of those servants came and settled accounts with them. So he who had received five talents came and brought five other talents, saying, 'Lord, you delivered to me five talents, look, I have gained five more talents besides them.' His lord said to him, "Well done, good and faithful servant; you were faithful over a few things, I will make you ruler over many things. Enter the joy of your Lord.

God created us; He knows our talents better than we do because He gave them to us. He expects us to use those talents to strengthen and help His kingdom grow. When we use those talents we receive the joy only God provides. When we use those talents we receive the joy only God provides.

Romans 15:13 Now may the God of hope fill you with all joy and peace in believing, that you may abound in hope by the power of the Holy Spirit.

We gain joy through God for many reasons. One is because we know God is strong enough to provide our physical needs. His strength is demonstrated in Matthew.

Matthew 14:19-21 Then He commanded the multitudes to sit down on the grass. And He took five loaves and two fish, and looking up to heaven, He blessed and broke and gave the loaves to the disciples; and the disciples gave to the multitudes. So they ate and were filled, and they took up twelve baskets full of the fragments that remained. Now those who had eaten were about 5,000 men beside women and children. God understands our physical needs.

He is strong enough to supply our needs. He knows how we can help the kingdom and He uses our skills when we are willing to serve.

John 10:10 The thief does not come except to steal, and to kill, and to destroy. I have come that they may have life, and that they may have it more abundantly.

Jesus tells us God's goal; it is so that we can have an abundant life. An example of the sisterhood we share through Christ and what that does for us is part of that abundant life.

Matthew 6:31:33 Therefore, do not worry, saying, "What shall we eat? Or what shall we drink? Or what shall we wear? For after all these things the Gentiles seek. For your heavenly Father knows that you need all these things. But seek first the kingdom of God and His righteousness, and all these things shall be added to you."

We must trust God to do what He has said He will do. This releases us from earthly worries that hinder our spiritual growth and joy. Recognizing God's role helps us prioritize those things that will bring us joy. Remember to be thankful! This is seen in Jesus' encounters with Mary, Martha, and Lazarus.

John 11:41 Then they took away the stone from the place where the dead man was lying. And Jesus lifted His eyes and said, "Father, I thank You that You have heard Me.

God gives us the talents, tools we need to obtain joy. He is our source of joy. He understands our needs, physical and spiritual and He is strong enough to provide for our needs. He listens to us and is our helper.

Psalm 54:4 Behold God is my helper; the Lord is with those who uphold my life.

God even helps others who He will use to help us. He does this even though God knows we are sinners.

Romans 3:23 For all have sinned and fall short of the glory of God.

He understands our weaknesses, so He offered a way for us to enter, or even re-enter His joy.

John 3:16 For God so loved the world that He gave His only begotten Son, that whoever believes in Him, should not perish but have everlasting life.

Knowing this we should be willing and motivated to do what God commands. We should obey even if the cost is suffering persecution for the cause of Christ.

1 Peter 4:12-14 Beloved, do not think it strange concerning the fiery trial which is to try you, as though some strange thing happened to you; but rejoice to the extent that you partake in Christ's sufferings, that when His glory is revealed, you may also be glad with exceeding joy. If you are reproached for the name of Christ, blessed are you, for the Spirit of glory and of God rests on you. On their part He is blasphemed, but on your part He is glorified.

We need to rejoice in the fact that God trusts us enough to give us opportunities to shine for Him. Rejoice that we have the chance to do something, however small, for God and Christ, who have both sacrificed so much for us. Then desire the opportunity to be a source of joy to God who gives us joy.

Knowing all we do about what God has done for us we want to bring joy to Him. Obeying God and even returning to Him brings Him joy.

3 John 4 I have no greater joy than to hear that my children walk in truth.

Luke 15:7 I say to you that likewise there will be more joy in heaven over one sinner that repents than over 99 just persons who need no repentance.

Our genuine faith in God brings Him joy.

I Peter 1:6-9 In this you greatly rejoice, though now for a little while, if need be, you have been grieved by various trials, that the genuineness of your faith, being much more precious than gold that perishes, though it is tested by fire, may be found to praise, honor, and glory at the revelation of Jesus Christ, whom having not seen you love. Though now you do not see Him, yet believing, you rejoice with joy inexpressible and full of glory, receiving the end of your faith – the salvation of your souls.

This is how we enter the joy of the Father: have faith, stand firm though we are tested, praise, honor, and glory that Jesus Christ is the Son of God and was sent for our salvation.

REFLECTION

1. This is Elfie, she could neither write or read when we met. The last time I was with her the previous year she had gestured for me to get a pen. I had not brought paper that year so we had written the books of the Bible on my arm and a linen laundry bag to help the women learn how to read and write. That night I thought Elfie wanted me to write something but she took the pen and through an interpreter told me that she wanted me to teach her how to write God's name in Chichewa, "Mulungu." When she was finished she showed off her hand where she had written God's name rejoicing with a joy that shone for all to see. This picture is when we first saw each other the next year. We greeted each other with a hug and she anxiously pointed to a piece of paper where she wrote and read from a Bible. Praise God!

Matthew 5:6 Blessed are those who hunger and thirst for righteousness. For they shall be filled.

We need to respect the truth enough not to change it. Verses teach us not to add or subtract from God's word.

Revelation 22:18-19 For I testify to everyone who hears the words of the prophesy of this book. If anyone adds to these things, God will add to him the plagues that are written in this book. If anyone takes away from the words of this book of this prophecy, God shall take away his part from the Book of Life, from the holy city and from the things which are written in this book.

One of the plagues this is talking about is the death of the firstborn in Exodus when God saved the Israelites.

Exodus 12:29-30 And it came to pass at midnight that the Lord struck all the firstborn in the land of Egypt, from the firstborn of Pharoah who sat on the throne to the firstborn of the captive who was in the dungeon, and all the firstborn of livestock. So Pharoah rose in the night, he, all his servants, and all the Egyptians; and there was a great cry in Egypt, for their was not a house where there was not one dead. And it came to pass at midnight that the Lord struck all the firstborn in the land of Egypt, from the firstborn of Pharoah who sat on the throne to the firstborn of the captive who was in the dungeon, and all the firstborn of livestock. So Pharoah rose in the night, he, all his servants, and all the Egyptians; and there was a great cry in Egypt, for their was not a house where there was not one dead.

If you are the firstborn of your family I would like you to recognize that had these instructions been given to our family and they were not followed we would have died. The fact is that any "gospel" that says something different than the Bible is not the word of God, and cannot save us.

Galatians 1:6-9 I marvel that you are turning away so soon from Him who called you in the grace of Christ, to a different gospel, which is not another, but there are some who trouble you and want to pervert the gospel of Christ. But even if we or an angel from heaven, preach any other gospel to you than what we have preached to you, let him be accursed. As we have said before, so I say again, of anyone preaches another gospel to you than what you have received let him be accursed.

Mormons often point out that the Book of Mormon was given by an angel. We are not here to dispute that. But what Paul says in Galatians means it does not matter if it was an angel who gave the text. It is different from the Bible and those who spread those teachings will be accursed. In the Old Testament, it says the same.

Deuteronomy 4:2 You shall not add to the word which I commanded you, nor take anything from it, that you may keep the commandments of the Lord your God which I commanded you.

We need to be serious about God's word. When the Israelites did God's word they were saved.

Jude 5 But I want to remind you, though you once knew this, that the Lord, having saved the people out of the land of Egypt, afterward destroyed those who did not believe.

When we ignore His word we will be punished.

Jude 11 Woe to them! For they have gone in the way of Cain, have run greedily in the error of Balaam for profit, and perished in the rebellion of Korah.

When we fully understand and appreciate the gifts God has given us we will pray for opportunities to share the truth.

2 John 3 Grace, mercy, and peace will be with you from God the Father and from the Lord Jesus Christ, the Son of the Father in truth and love.

John rejoiced because of those who stood.

v. 4 I rejoiced greatly that I have found some of your children walking in truth, as we received commandment from the Father.

God's word demands we walk in love with each other, that means sharing the truth.

v. 6 This is love, that we walk according to His commandments.

This is the commandment to you, that which we have heard from the beginning: that we love one another.

Learn how to love from God's word.

v. 7 This is love, that we walk according to His commandments. This is the commandment, that as you have heard from the beginning, you should walk it.

REFLECTION

2. In Acts 2:42-47 we are told that after those who believed and were baptized were added to the church by God enjoyed fellowship going from house-to-house breaking bread. The hospitality that is shown in Malawi is humbling. In America we are often concerned we do not have a nice enough home, or good enough food to extend hospitality. That is not a biblical principle. We witnessed the greatest hospitality sitting on uneven wooden benches, eating meat that was not readily identifiable, and eating

rice that they could not afford to feed themselves. Eating this while the women who worked over open fires to prepare the food ate corn flour they had ground mixed with water, sima.

In one village, I was invited to join the women where they ate after the meal while the men visited and it was an animal pen. I went, and much to their surprise joined in the chore of washing the dishes. A humorous, sister-building moment ensued when I started washing dishes, sitting on my knees in the dirt. Their giggles of joy and amazement that I knew how to wash dishes and would not let them help me clean up after they had cooked developed a bond between us that will last forever. Oh to be humble as to willingly share food when little food is available and to work over a fire with no appliances to help with the preparation to fix food that I am deemed not worthy to eat. That is hospitality, and these are the women who taught me that.

CHAPTER 7

BEING A GODLY WOMAN
Kukhala Mkazi woopa Mulungu

God tells us all to live godly lives.

Titus 2:11-13 For the grace of God that bringeth salvation hath appeared to all men, teaching us that, denying ungodliness and worldly lusts, we should live soberly, righteously, and godly, in this present world. Looking for that blessed hope, and the glorious appearing of the great God and our Savior Jesus Christ;

He also tells us that He will teach us how to do what asks us to do.

Proverbs 3:5 Trust in the Lord with all your heart, and do not lean on your own understanding. In all your ways acknowledge Him, and He will make straight your paths.

That is why it is important that we go to the Bible to see what God says to women about how to live godly in His sight. One way we can live godly is as a wife.

1 Peter 3:1 Likewise, ye wives, be in subjection to your own husbands; that, if any obey not the word, they also may without the word be won by the conversation of the wives.

When we are wives that live by the standards that God sets, like being in submission we can help save our husbands from the devil. Submission to our husbands is part of our role but, how else are we to live?

Titus 2:3-5 The aged women likewise, that they be in behavior as becometh holiness, not false accusers, not given to much wine, teachers of good things; That they may teach the younger to be sober, to love their husbands, to love their children, to be discreet, chaste, keepers at home, good, obedient to their own husbands, that the word of God be not blasphemed.

Women are to love, God defines what love is.

1 Corinthians 13:4-8 Love suffered long, and is kind; charity envies not; charity vaunteth not itself, is not puffed up, Doth not behave itself unseemly, seeketh not its own, is not easily provoked, thinketh no evil; Rejoiceth not in iniquity, but rejoiceth in the truth; Beareth all things, believeth all things, hopeth all things, endureth all things. Love never faileth…

How we are to love?

Love suffered long this means an "extended, long time." When Peter asked Jesus how many times he had to forgive someone that sinned against him Jesus answered in Matthew.

Matthew 18:21-22 Then came Peter to him, and said, Lord, how oft shall my brother sin against me, and I forgive him? Till seven times? Jesus saith unto him, "I say not unto thee, Until seven times: but, until seventy times seven.

Jesus told Peter to be willing to forgive someone 490 times in a day. Am I willing to forgive that often?

Love is Kind: that means "full of service to others."

Philippians 2:3 Let nothing be done through strife or vainglory; but in lowliness of mind let each esteem other better than themselves.

Everything we do should be for the good of others. Not putting myself and my desires first, but instead putting others first *and myself last.*

I Corinthians 13 also says love does not envy. Do I complain about the same things to God repeatedly because I think someone else has it easier than me, or are better off than me? Instead, I should pray to God and trust Him to take care of me and the concerns I have. Our attitude must be one of humility.

James 4:10 Humble yourselves before the Lord, and He will exalt you.

When we do God's will, He will reward us more than any man could ever reward us. God stresses humility.

Matthew 23:5 But all their works they do to be seen by men… Instead, He says, "But he who is greatest among you shall be your servant. And whoever exalts himself will be humbled, and he who humbles himself will be exalted."

REFLECTION

1. In Kajuni Village we would be fed in the chief's home where he had borrowed chairs for us to sit at a borrowed table. The women could be seen fixing the meal hours prior and the woman you see with me at the wash tub would get up each morning and sweep away any debris from the center of the village with a grass hand broom. After each meal I would gather up the dishes and scurry, that is about as fast as I can run, to the wash tub. The chief would call after me and the women would try to get me to stop washing the dishes because I was their guest and teacher.

After one lesson where we talked about the older women teaching the younger women and how Ruth listened to Naomi the older woman, this friend followed me to the tub. She took the dishes from my hands and pointed at me and then herself and her ear. The interpreter soon came and explained. She was telling me that she was older and that I was younger, so I had to follow the Bible and listen to her. I was no longer able to wash the dishes. I was stunned, and befuddled, how could I refuse to do what I taught when the women were already applying the lessons they learned from the Bible.

God also says love does not to act unseemly: "improperly" or "dishonorably." God gives us examples of this.

1 Corinthians 14:34-36 Let your women keep silent in the churches, for they are not permitted to speak; but they are to be submissive, as the law also says.

It is unseemly for a woman to take a public leadership role in the church or family.

1 Corinthians 11:3 But I would have you know that the head of every man is Christ; and the head of the woman is the man; and the head of Christ is God.

Our submission in our relationships demonstrate our love of God. God's instructions must come first.

Luke 14:25-27 And there went great multitudes with Him: and He turned and said unto them, If any man come to Me, and hate not his father, and mother, and wife, and children, and brethren, and sisters, yea, and his own life also, he cannot be my disciple. And whosoever doth not bear his cross, and come after me, cannot be my disciple.

Going back to *Titus 2:3-5* which says,

The aged women likewise, that they be in behavior as becometh holiness, not false accusers, not given to much wine, teachers of good things; That they may teach the younger to be sober, to love their husbands, to love their children, to be discreet, keepers at home, good, obedient to their own husbands, that the word of God be not blasphemed.

We see that many of the things we are to do, or not to do, involve what we say. For example, older women are to teach. That does not mean only the oldest women teach. We all have a responsibility to help other, less experienced women, learn the skills we were once taught.

There are also serious warnings here in Titus. God says we are to be discreet, which means self-controlled in the mind and not to be a false accuser.

Proverbs 6:16-19 These six things doth the LORD hate: yea, seven are an abomination unto him: A proud look, a lying tongue, and hands that shed innocent blood, An heart that deviseth wicked imaginations, feet that be swift in running to mischief, A false witness that speaketh lies, and he that soweth discord among brethren.

In this verse, there are seven things in this world that God hates and considers an abomination. Four of those are a lying tongue, devising wicked imaginations, a false witness, and someone who stirs up trouble among brethren. Those same four things are listed in Titus as things older women are supposed to teach younger women. How important does that make our job to teach those things to others?

John 13:35 35 By this shall all men know that ye are my disciples, if ye have love one to another.

Godly women submit to God and thus our husbands and to men in public worship. Godly women love the way God describes in 1 Corinthians 13, and they use their voice to teach others how to please God. And when we are godly women we will one day hear God say…

Matthew 25:21 His lord said unto him, Well done, thou good and faithful servant: thou hast been faithful over a few things, I will make thee ruler over many things: enter thou into the joy of thy Lord.

REFLECTION

2. We received our schedule for the 2022 trip days prior to leaving. This didn't surprise us as Malawi time is very different than American time but we were facing a challenge. Some of the elders in Malawi had decided to have what we would call a gospel meeting, or revival for women. This was significant for many reasons, one being that invitations went out across the country and over 22 congregations would be represented, some even coming from Mozambique. Next, we had Bibles to distribute because of the kindness of members of churches of Christ, not to be mistaken for the church of Latter-Day Saints, across America.

While many welcomed us, the next challenge came from an unforeseen source, there were those in Malawi who had been teaching that it was not biblical for women to teach other women in Bible classes, that only men could teach them. I kindly suggested that they consult *Titus 2:3-4.* And while the question was answered this did not ensure that there would not be those who would be present disputing the validity of our meeting.

Logistics also provided a hurdle, we were supposed to fly in on Friday, arriving in the mid-afternoon, and this year Jessie and Ella, a mother-daughter team, were accompanying us for part of the journey. They had not taught in Malawi and had yet to experience the fluidity of the scheduling associated with teaching in Malawi. The conference was scheduled, invitations sent out, and the times that we were to teach, and the topics they wanted covered were changed. That in-and-of-itself would be a challenge without the fact that we had a 24-hour flight, 9-hour time change, and were supposed to teach less than 24 hours later. The crowd was nearly 700 women and the three of us combined taught, worshiped, and sang for seven hours. None of these hurdles could have been surpassed if God had not been on our side.

Jessie, Ella and I worshipping with the women in Malawi.

CHAPTER 8

GOD'S PLANS FOR US
Zolinga Za Mulungu kwa Lfe

Jerimiah 29:11 For I know the plans I have for you, declares the Lord, plans to prosper you and not to harm you, plans to give you hope and a future.

We need to trust that God knows and wants what is best for us. Sometimes we do not because we lean on our own understanding of situations.

Proverbs 3:5-6 Trust in the Lord with all thine heart, and lean not unto thine own understanding in all thy ways acknowledge Him, and He shall direct thy paths.

In the Old Testament, we see an example of two sisters. One was Leah, who saw God working in her life and the other was Rachel who focused on what the world could give her.

Leah and Rachel were Laban's daughters who each married Jacob, a patriarch blessed by God. Those promises are recorded.

Genesis 28:14 And thy seed shall be as the dust of the earth, and thou shalt spread abroad to the west, and to the east, and to the north, and to the south: and in thee and in thy seed shall all the families of the earth be blessed.

God fulfilled those promises through Leah and Rachel, Jacob's wives who were also sisters. The Bible introduces us to them in *Gen 29:16.*

Laban had two daughters: the name of the elder was Leah, and the name of the younger was Rachel. Leah was tender-eyed, but Rachel was beautiful and well-formed.

These are the differences we see in the sisters.

1. Leah was tender eyed, or as we would say tender hearted a trait required of us today.

Ephesians 4:32 And be ye kind one to another, tenderhearted, forgiving one another even as God, for Christ's sake hath forgiven you.

Rachel was beautiful and favored traits the world says are important but what does God say?

1 Samuel 16:7 But the Lord said unto Samuel, look not on his countenance, or on the height of his stature, because I have refused him; because I have refused him; for the Lord seeth not as man seeth; for man looketh on the outward appearance, but the Lord looketh on the heart.

Genesis 29:30-30:1 And he, Jacob, went in also unto Rachel, and he also loved Rachel more than Leah, and served with him (Laban) yet 7 other years. And when the Lord saw that Leah was hated, he opened her womb; but Rachel was barren.

Leah was favored by God.

Isaiah 66:2 For all those things hath mine hand made, and all those things have been, saith the Lord: but to this man will I look, Even to him that is poor and contrite spirit, and trembleth at My word.

Genesis 30:8 And Rachel said, with great wrestlings have I wrestled with my sister, and I have prevailed, and she called his name, Naphtali.

Psalm 36:2 For he flattereth himself in his own eyes until his iniquity be found to be hateful. The words of his mouth are inequity and deceit; he have left off to be wise, and to do good.

Rachel was favored by man and in her own eyes.

God talks about people who flatter themselves.

Psalm 36:2-3 For he flatters himself in his own eyes. When he finds out his iniquity and when he hates. The words of his mouth are wickedness and deceit; they fail to act.

2. Leah trusted God and recognized His hand in her life.

Genesis 29:32-35
v. 32 God sees
v. 33 God heard
v. 35 I will praise God

Rachel tried to work around God.

Genesis 30:3 And Rachel said, Behold my maid, Bilhah go into her, and she shall bear upon my knees that I may also have children by her.

Leah focused on her blessings.

Genesis 30:11 Then Leah said," a troop comes!" So she called his name Gad.

Rachel focused on herself.

Genesis 30:1 Now when Rachel saw that she bore Jacob no children, Rachel envied her sister, and said to Jacob, "Give me children or else I die!

Genesis 30:14 Now Reuben went in the days of wheat harvest and found mandrakes in the field, and brought them to his mother Leah. Then Rachel said to Leah, "Please give me some of your son's mandrakes."

Genesis 30:8 With great wrestlings, I have wrestled with my sister, and indeed I have prevailed.

3. Leah obeyed without deceit, both God and man, her husband.

Genesis 30:20 And Leah said, "God has endowed me with a good endowment; now my husband will dwell with me, because I have born him six sons. And she called his name Zebulun.

Genesis 33:2-3 Now Jacob lifted his eyes and looked, and there, Esau was coming, and with him were 400 men. So he divided the children of Leah, Rachel and the 2 maidservants. And he put the maidservants and their children in front, Leah, and her children behind, and Rachel and Joseph last.

When Jacob left Esau's presence, Esau vowed He would kill Jacob. So when Jacob is going back to see Esau he is afraid of what Esau might do. So Jacob arranges his family from least important to him, to most important, in case some are killed. In all the times that Leah is shown she is not as loved as Rachel. God never mentions a time where Leah complained to God or Jacob, or tried to deceitfully gain favor.

Rachel stole, deceived, and put her desires first.

Genesis 31:34 Now Rachel had taken the household idols, put them in the camel's saddle, and sat on them. And Laban searched all about the tent but did not find them. And she said to her father, "Let it not displease my lord that I cannot rise before thee, for the manner of women is with me. And he searched but did not find the idols.

According to today's society, Rachel had it all:

a. Physical beauty
b. Favor/love of her father and husband
c. Status

Leah on the other hand should be pitied but what does God think?

a. God saw Leah's heart

1 Samuel 16:7 But the Lord said to Samuel "Do not look on his appearance or at the height of his stature, because I have refused him. For the Lord does not see as man sees; for man looks at the outward appearance, but the Lord looks at the heart.

b. God gave Leah a position she would not have had if she remained single and childless.

Romans 8:28 And we know that all things work together for good to those who love God, to those who are called according to His purpose.

Think of the love Leah was given through her children.

c. Leah was content. We can see that in the names of her children. God sees, God gave me a good dowry, happy am I, God heard, Reward will come, now Jacob will dwell with me, I will praise the Lord, vindicated, daughters called me blessed.

James 1:16-17 Do not be deceived, my beloved brethren. Every good gift and every perfect gift is from above, and comes down from the Father of lights, with whom there is no variation or shadow of turning.

Leah is a matriarch, the true Israel. Judah comes from her and Jesus does as well. She is our example of not taking revenge.

Matthew 1:2 Shows Leah's son Judah was in the genealogy of Jesus.

1 Thessalonians 5:15-18 See that no one renders evil for evil to anyone, but always pursue what is good both for yourselves and all Rejoicing always, pray without ceasing, in everything give thanks; for this is the will of God in Christ Jesus for you.

d. Leah was honored as first wife at the time of her death.

Genesis 49:29-31 Then he (Jacob) charged them and said to them, "I am to be gathered to my people, bury me with my fathers in the cave that is in the field of Ephron the Hittite, in the cave that is in the field of Machpaleh, which is before Mamre in the land of Canaan, which Abraham bought with the field of Ephron the Hittite as a possession for a burial place. There they buried Abraham and Sarah his wife, there they buried Isaac and Rebekah his wife, and there I buried Leah.

Leah shows a heart that is tender and surrenders to God is more important than outward beauty and the standards of the world.

Proverbs 31:30-31 Charm is deceitful and beauty is vain, but a woman who fears the Lord she shall be praised. Give her of the fruit of her hands and let her own works praise her in the gates.

REFLECTION

One of the lessons we quickly learned that day was that the Bible is timeless.

James 2:2-4 "For if there come unto your assembly a man with a gold ring, in goodly apparel, and there come in also a poor man in vile raiment; and ye have respect to him that weareth the gay clothing, and say unto him, Sit thou here in a good place; and say to the poor, Stand thou there, or sit here under my footstool: Are ye not then partial in yourselves, and are become judges of evil thoughts?"

There was not a building large enough to hold the women who traveled to worship and learn that day. There was not even enough food to feed everyone. The result was a deference was shown to the poorer women like those who are addressed in James. It broke our hearts. Along with the Bibles pens and paper had been brought from America to give to those who did not have the tools to take notes because of the cost or the lack of availability in the villages. When they were passed out at the beginning of the lessons women were encouraged to only take supplies if they did not have their own.

What we saw became a trend among many of the groups. Women who had pens would put them away and then take one of those brought from America because of the status that had been assigned the supplies from abroad. The selfishness even extended to the distribution of the Bibles, some who already had God's word were asking for new Bibles even though they knew that would mean some sisters who did not have a copy of God's word would not receive one. The righteous indignation that Jesus showed in the temple when He saw the money changers became much more understandable to me that day and throughout our trip. (*Matthew 21:12-13*.) The lesson was developed after we saw prejudicial treatment of the poorer sisters and thankfully brought repentance to many.

CHAPTER 9

THE EVILS OF PREJUDICE
Zoipa Zatsankho

Over the years that we have come to Malawi, we have witnessed prejudice, and a lack of love towards others when it comes to these matters, it has broken our hearts and angered God. So, I come speaking as Paul asked Timothy to admonish and rebuke those practices.

When Paul was talking to Timothy, a young preacher, he taught how to teach the word, he said to teach in Season and out of season. That is found in *2 Timothy 4:2.* Paul said to reprove, rebuke, exhort with all longsuffering and doctrine. Today I am here to do that.

The ministry in Malawi is a great blessing but like the churches mentioned in the Bible there are challenges (Revelation 2 and 3). In Malawi those who are poor, according to the world's standards, are treated with disdain. This prejudice sets up a hierarchy that displeases God.

Colossians 3:11 where there is neither Greek nor Jew, circumcised nor uncircumcised, barbarian, Scythian, slave nor free, but Christ is all and in all.

In God's family, we are not to look at nationality, past religious practice, education, or the monetary status of our brothers and sisters in order to decide how we should treat each other. Jesus did not treat others with partiality, and He expects us to follow His example in that.

Miriam judged Moses' wife as unworthy because she was a Shulamite. In *Exodus 2:21* it says that, *Then Moses was content to live with the man, and he gave Zipporah his daughter to*

Moses. Miriam's attitude made God so angry that he struck her with leprosy.

Numbers 12:12 Please do not let her be as one dead, whose flesh is half consumed when he comes out of his mother's womb!

Do we really want to do something that will make God that angry? James, the brother of Jesus, wrote about how Jesus felt about honoring people because of their wealth.

James 2:1-9 My brethren, do not hold the faith of our Lord Jesus Christ, the Lord of glory, with partiality. For if there should come into your assembly a man with gold rings, in fine apparel, and there should also come in a poor man in filthy clothes, and you pay attention to the one wearing the fine clothes and say to him, "You sit here in a good place," and say to the poor man, "You stand there," or, "Sit here at my footstool," have you not shown partiality among yourselves, and become judges with evil thoughts?

Listen, my beloved brethren: Has God not chosen the poor of this world to be rich in faith and heirs of the kingdom which He promised to those who love Him? But you have dishonored the poor man. Do not the rich oppress you and drag you into the courts? Do they not blaspheme that noble name by which you are called?

If you really fulfill the royal law according to the Scripture, "You shall love your neighbor as yourself," you do well; but if you show partiality, you commit sin, and are convicted by the law as transgressors.

Let's use an example of this today. My sisters don't give the seats of honor to those who are from the cities and have great wealth, position, and fine garments. Don't tell the village women to sit outside on the ground so that the wealthy may see the speaker during the presentation. Don't give the wealthy the meat and rice and then provide only sima those from the villages. When you receive Bibles do not give them to those who already possess a bible or a way to purchase one. When you pass out paper and pens so that we can learn, don't take from those who have nothing.

Acts 10:34-35 Then Peter opened his mouth and said: "In truth I perceive that God shows no partiality. But in every nation whoever fears Him and works righteousness is accepted by Him.

God has servants of all nationalities, do not judge people because they are from Mozambique, Zambia, or the villages of Malawi. Do not elevate those from America; instead, test every word that we teach to make sure it is from God.

Acts 13:1 Now in the church that was at Antioch there were certain prophets and teachers: Barnabas, Simeon who was called Niger, Lucius of Cyrene, Manaen who had been brought up with Herod the Tetrarch, and Saul.

God made us all.

Acts 17:26 And He has made from one blood every nation of men to dwell on all the face of the earth, and has determined their preappointed times and the boundaries of their dwellings.

REFLECTION

Every culture struggles with prejudice because it is a common people problem, even within the church. One service, we had an attendance that topped 1500 people, 1200 were women. As the sermons ended the women were told by the elders they would continue their studies in a class while the men went outside and ate. The picture above is from this gathering.

It was not long after the men received their food they started standing outside the building where they were seen encouraging the women to leave the building so they could have some place to sit and eat out of the sun. Notice there is no glass in the windows and the women are sitting on a dirt floor. These demands were especially distracting because there was no buffer between the men and the women and then Malawi culture came into play. As one Christian brother explained in Malawi, if a man tells a woman to jump they say, "How many times?"

After cutting the Bible lesson in half we left the building and resumed our "rightful place" in the sun. The culture in Malawi is said to be womanizing, scores laugh when that is said. The fact is, the word womanizing does not begin to explain the servitude that has been established in the country of men demanding service without extending the love Ephesians 5 demands of husbands. But this day we saw something even more discouraging. Women, who had prepared food for the hoards, were skipped in the distribution of the food, much like Acts 7. The result was groups who ate Malawi delicacies while others had nothing. Groups even forced sima, a simple corn flour and water dough, into their mouths rather than sharing with those who had none.

I went and sat on the ground with one group who was not being fed. The children and I learned Bible school songs while the older women watched. I was horrified, they were starving and frankly, God was enraged. How often do we consider I Corinthians 11 and those who were eating meals in front of their

Christian sisters who had less or none but think it is something that was a problem. Jesus said it is harder for a rich person to be saved than for a camel to go through the eye of a needle (*Matthew 19:23-26*). We pray for our Malawi sisters, and those across the globe, that we will not allow Satan to purchase our hearts with physical riches.

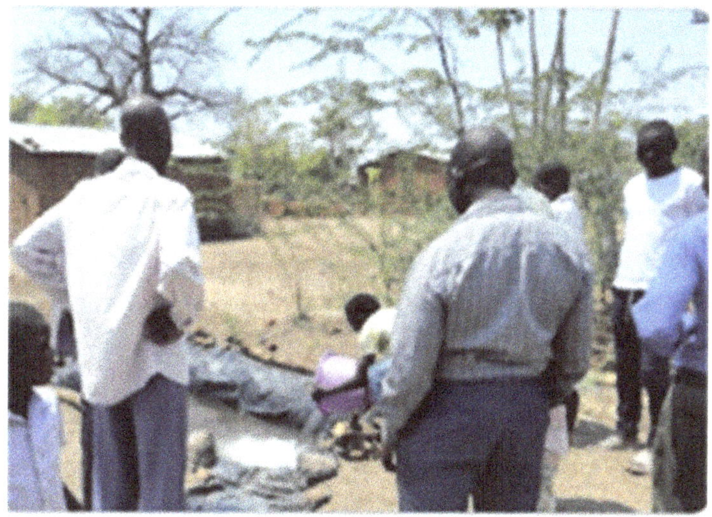

This young woman is transporting water to a whole that was dug and covered with a tarp to make a baptistry. She has done what she can.

CHAPTER 10

GOD'S SPIRITUAL WOMEN
Akazi auzimu a Mulungu

We are to be lights of the world Matthew 5:14-16

You are the light of the world a city that is set on a hill cannot be hidden. Nor do they light a lamp and put it under a basket, but on a lampstand, and it gives light to all who are in the house. Let your light so shine before men, that they may see your good works and glorify your Father in heaven.

God expects us to be hard workers, Colossians 3:23.

Whatsoever ye do, do it heartily, as to the Lord, not unto men.

It is important that we learn about God, Luke 10:38-42.

Now it came to pass, as they went, that he entered a certain village: and a certain woman named Martha received him into her house. And she had a sister called Mary, which also sat at Jesus' feet, and heard his word. But Martha was cumbered about much serving, and came to him, and said, Lord, dost thou not care that my sister hath left me to serve alone? Bid her therefore that she helps me. And Jesus answered and said unto her, Martha, Martha, thou art careful and troubled about many things: But one thing is needful; and Mary hath chosen that good part, which shall not be taken away from her.

As sisters, mothers, and grandmothers we have an opportunity to leave a godly legacy in our families, *2 Timothy 1:3-5*.

I thank God, whom I serve with a pure conscience, as my forefathers did, as without ceasing I remember you in my prayers night and day, greatly desiring to see you, being mindful of your tears, that I may be filled with joy, when I call to remembrance the genuine faith that is in you, which dwelt first in your grandmother Lois and your mother Eunice, and I am persuaded in you also.

One of the legacies that we teach is that we should love other Christians, *I John 2:9-11.*

He that saith he is in the light, and hateth his brother, is in darkness even until now. He that loveth his brother abideth in the light, and there is none occasion of stumbling in him. But he that hateth his brother is in darkness, and walketh in darkness, and knoweth not whether he goeth, because that darkness hath blinded his eyes.

One of the ways that we demonstrate our love for others is to teach those who believe a scriptural error, *Acts 18:24-26.*

And a certain Jew named Apollos, born at Alexandria, and eloquent man, and mighty in the scriptures, came to Ephesus. This man was instructed in the way of the Lord; and being fervent in the spirit, he spoke and taught diligently the things of the Lord, knowing only the baptism of John. And he began to speak boldly in the synagogue: when Aquila and Priscilla had heard, they took him unto them, and expounded unto him the way of God more perfectly.

We need to trust God, which is developed through reading His word.

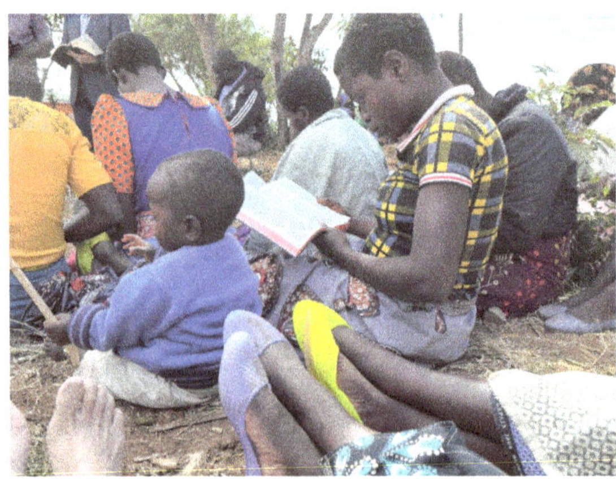

James 1:17 Every good and perfect gift is from above, coming down from the Father of the heavenly lights, with whom there is no change or shifting shadow.

Humility allows us to put ourselves in the position God wants us to be in to serve, *Ephesians 4:2.*

Be completely humble and gentle; be patient, bearing with one another in love.

Humility naturally leads to unselfishness, *Philippians 2:4-6.*

Everyone should look not to his own interests, but also to the interests of others. Let this mind be in you which was also in Christ Jesus: Who, existing in the form of God, did not consider equality with God something to be grasped.

Matthew 16:24 Then Jesus told His disciples, "If anyone wants to come after Me, he must deny himself and take up his cross and follow Me.

God also desires that we are content with our physical blessings, I Timothy 6:6-7.

Of course, godliness with contentment is great gain. For we brought nothing into the world, so we cannot carry anything out of it.

Luke 12:15 And He said to them, "Watch out! Guard yourselves against every form of greed, for one's life does not consist in the abundance of his possessions.

So what are the results of doing what God says?

1. Praise and recognition from family

Proverbs 31:27Her children rise and call her blessed; her husband praises her as well.

Proverbs 31:30 Charm is deceitful and beauty is vain but a woman who serves the Lord shall be praised.

2. Husband's trust and contentment

Proverbs 31:11 The heart of her husband trusts in her, and he lacks nothing of value.

3. A worth far above rubies.

Proverbs 31:10 A wife of noble character, who can find? She is far more precious than rubies.

4. Wisdom

Proverbs 31:26 She opens her mouth with wisdom, and faithful instruction is on her tongue.

James 1:5 If any of you lacks wisdom, let him ask God, who gives generously to all without reproach, and it will be given him.

REFLECTION

Some of the smallest groups showed the greatest love and zeal for our Lord. The willingness of these women to take turns working so that they could all hear part of God's word was an example to us all. Here is what Becky took away from Malawi, It has always been in my heart to travel overseas and help spread the Good News. It never seemed like the right timing. When Misti and Wendell moved to Phoenix, I got to know Misti and she talked about going to Malawi. It felt like this was the opportunity I had been looking for. Here I am Lord…send me was running through my head. It was time to allow the Lord to use me and trust Him. It took a huge leap of faith and trust in Him to fly there alone and then get to work.

CHAPTER 11

STANDING IN THE BREACH
Kuyimirira mu Kuphwanya

REFLECTION

One day, when Becky had joined us in Malawi my husband was sick so Shadreck, Larry, Becky, and I filed into the truck and headed toward the Zambia border. The congregation that we went to was new and members from another group were gathering with them. We wanted to make sure and bring Bibles and supplies to help the fledgling group. Afterward, we were awaiting the men, which to be honest rarely happened. And when the need arose we took turns going to the chimbuzi, restroom. Becky was first and made the discovery that there was no wall on the other side of the stall to shield her from the workers who were coming from Zambia, males who were inebriated. The woman in the yellow and brown wrap came to our rescue, placing her wrap on the grass walls to hide us from these men. Afterwards, I was "feeling my oats' ' and asked Becky if she wanted to walk to the truck instead of having them drive up to us and she agreed. While I was waiting for Becky one of the workers walked over to me and spoke in Chichewa, he was noticeably surprised when I replied in their tongue. Then Becky joined us, and we started down the mountain path. Soon there were five workers instead of one and they were speaking in English after the one explained I spoke Chichewa. They were up to no good and it was evident, we later found out that women were sometimes kidnapped, taken over the Zambia border. A couple more steps into our walk I slipped on a stone and our nervousness was real. But to our surprise, and the workers we were soon surrounded by the women in this picture. They had watched us and came to stand in the breach, protecting us from evil.

To stand in the breach is to put ourselves between a danger and someone or something that we care about. We do that for our families and God expects us to do that for His people as well. The Jewish midwives, Shiphra and Puah, saved the male babies from Pharoah.

Exodus 1:15, 16, 20, 21 Then the king of Egypt spoke to the Hebrew midwives, of whom the name of one was Shiphrah and the name of the other Puah; and he said, "When you do the duties of a midwife for the Hebrew women and see them on the birthstools if it is a son, then you shall kill him; but if it is a daughter, then she shall live" But the midwives feared God and did not do as the king of Egypt commanded them, but saved the male children alive. Therefore, God dealt well with the midwives, and the people multiplied and grew very mighty. And so it was, because the midwives feared God, that He provided households for them.

In *Joshua 2:1-11* we meet an unlikely heroine, Rahab. A Canaanite woman, harlot by trade, had seen the power of God and decided to stand for Him and His people instead of her own.

And Joshua the son of Nun sent out of Shittim two men to spy secretly, saying, Go view the land, even Jericho. And they went, and came into an harlot's house, named Rahab, and lodged there. And it was told the king of Jericho, saying, Behold, there came men in hither to night of the children of Israel to search out the country. And the king of Jericho sent unto Rahab, saying, Bring forth the men that are come to thee, which are entered into thine house: for they be come to search out all the country. And the woman took the two men, and hid them, and said thus, There came men unto me, but I wist not whence they were: And it came to pass about the time of shutting of the gate, when it was dark, that the men went out: whither the men went I wot not: pursue after them quickly; for ye shall overtake them. But she had brought them up to the roof of the house, and hid them with the stalks of flax, which she had laid in order upon the roof. And the men pursued after them the way to Jordan unto the fords: and as soon as they which pursued after them were gone out, they shut the gate. And before they were laid down, she came up unto them upon the roof; And she said unto the men, I know that the Lord hath given you the land, and that your terror is fallen upon us, and that all the inhabitants of the land faint because of you. For we have heard how the Lord dried up the water of the Red sea for you, when ye came out of Egypt; and what ye did unto the two kings of the Amorites, that were on the other side Jordan, Sihon and Og, whom ye utterly destroyed. And as soon as we had heard these things, our hearts did melt, neither did there remain any more courage in any man, because of you: for the Lord your God, he is God in heaven above, and in earth beneath.

If God can use Rahab to save His people He can use us all! We only need to be willing to see His works and trust Him so that we can stand in the breach. This may be hard at times but consider, God used Rahab, a harlot, and she became the grandmother of David and the great… grandmother of Jesus. God rewards those who stand in the breach.

Deborah, the prophetess and judge trusted God and went to battle with Barak, a man who didn't have faith in God, defeating Sisera, a renown commander in Judges 4:4-8.

And Deborah, a prophetess, the wife of Lapidoth, she judged Israel at that time. And she dwelt under the palm tree of Deborah between Ramah and Bethel in mount Ephraim: and the children of Israel came up to her for judgment. And she sent and called Barak the son of Abinoam out of Kedeshnaphtali, and said unto him, Hath not the Lord God of Israel commanded, saying, Go and draw toward mount Tabor, and take with thee ten thousand men of the children of Naphtali and of the children of Zebulun? And I will draw unto thee to the river Kishon Sisera, the captain of Jabin's army, with his chariots and his multitude; and I will deliver him into thine hand. And Barak said unto her, If thou wilt go with me, then I will go: but if thou wilt not go with me, then I will not go.

Priscilla prepared to help teach and was willing to risk her life ministering to the churches of the Gentiles. In *Acts 18:24-26...*

Now a certain Jew named Apollos, born at Alexandria, an eloquent man and mighty in the Scriptures, came to Ephesus. This man had been instructed in the way of the Lord, and being fervent in spirit, he spoke and taught the things of the Lord accurately, though he knew only the baptism of John. So he began to speak boldly in the synagogue. When Aquila and Priscilla heard him, they took him aside and explained to him the way of God more accurately.

Romans 16:3-5 Greet Priscilla and Aquila, my fellow workers in Christ Jesus, who risked their own necks for my life, to whom not only I give thanks, but also all the churches of the Gentiles. Likewise, greet the church that is in their house. Mary took care of missionaries.

Romans 16:6 Greet Mary, who bestowed much labour on us

— Performed many good offices for the faithful, especially for the preachers of the gospel.

Women are to teach those who are younger than them, both physically and spiritually.

Titus 2:3 The older women likewise, that they may be reverent in behavior, not slanderers, not given to much wine, teachers of good things.

Dorcas gave us an example when she stood in the breach for the poor and the widows by helping them in their need. *Acts 9:37-41...*

At Joppa, there was a certain disciple named Tabitha, which is translated as Dorcas. This woman was full of good works and charitable deeds, which she did. But it happened in those days that she became sick and died. When they had washed her, they laid her in an upper room. And since Lydda was near Joppa, and the disciples had heard that Peter was there, they sent two men to him, imploring him not to delay in coming to them. Then Peter arose and went with them. When he had come, they brought him to the upper room. And all the widows stood by him weeping, showing the tunics and garments which Dorcas had made while she was with them. But Peter put them all out and knelt and prayed. And turning to the body, he said, "Tabitha, rise." And she opened her eyes, and when she saw Peter, she sat up. Then he gave her his hand and lifted her up; and when he had called the saints and widows, he presented her alive.

God used Dorcas/Tabitha to help those in need. We need to do what we can to help those, especially our brothers and sisters in Christ, today. In *2 Timothy 1:5* we hear of Eunice and Louis teaching their family and providing a preacher to the world, Timothy.

REFLECTION

Shadrack Nyambo is one such preacher, a gentle giant who gave up earthly power and position to serve the Lord. He is our driver, handyman, interpreter, protector, standing in the breach and preacher whose heart is focused on bringing God's word to his home, Malawi. He is our Barnabas, facing the requests of many, ensuring that God's help is distributed God's way (Acts 4:32-36, Acts 11:22-24).

The work in Malawi is supported by many, including those who travel to the country to teach children while the women are learning how to study their new Bibles. That is what Melanie Travis did and her willingness to do so allowed us to teach approximately 6,000 women during our 2023 trip.

2 Timothy 1:5-7 when I call to remembrance the genuine faith that is in you, which dwelt first in your grandmother Lois and your mother Eunice, and I am persuaded is in you also. Therefore, I remind you to stir up the gift of God which is in you through the laying on of my hands. For God has not given us a spirit of fear, but of power and of love and of a sound mind.

Jesus came to stand in the breach and save us from our sins; we then must stand up for our fellow Christians and help protect and provide for them so we can make it to heaven.

Becky Thayer expresses it this way, I was excited to go out and meet the people and help pass out Bibles. I had a lesson prepared about how to pray with some backup plans and extras in case of an 'emergency.' I will never forget the joy on the faces of the women as we met with them. They were welcoming and so excited to hear from the Word of God. The women taught me what service looks like. Working tirelessly and with joy to prepare food and make us visitors feel welcome. They hungered for the word and listened intently to everything that was said. There were times I pulled the children out to teach them some simple lessons. It is hard to talk about it without tearing up because they listened so intently and wanted more. They didn't want the lessons to stop.

After teaching the women in one village, we walked to meet the men, and as we walked, the women started singing. It was the most beautiful thing I had ever witnessed. Pure joy and love for God. It was a glimpse of what heaven will be like. Walking hand in hand, all singing praises together. Malawi taught me to remember to be hungry for the word. It taught me to be joyful in all circumstances. Every single face I looked at there is etched in my heart. I saw God in each of them. I saw hope. I saw a hunger to know Him better. It challenged me to dig deeper and be prepared with an answer for everything. I cannot wait to go back and work with the women and children.

CHAPTER 12

HOW TO GLORIFY GOD
Momwe Mungalemekezere Mulungu

There are many ways society says we should glorify God, but He is very specific on how we should do this. The first thing He tells us to do is to produce fruit.

John 15:8 By this My Father is glorified, that you bear much fruit; so you will be My disciples.

This is not physical fruit, it is spiritual fruit like we read in *Galatians 5:22-23. But the fruit of the Spirit is love, joy, peace, forbearance, kindness, goodness, faithfulness, gentleness, and self-control. Against such things there is no law. So, when we show these traits to others we are glorifying God.*

Romans 15:5-6 Now may the God of patience and comfort grant you to be like-minded toward one another, according to Christ Jesus, that you may with one mind and one mouth glorify the God and Father of our Lord Jesus Christ.

We need to work, peacefully, for the good of God's kingdom.

1 Corinthians 6:19-20 Or do you not know that your body is the temple of the Holy Spirit who is in you, whom you have from God, and you are not your own? For you were bought at a price; therefore glorify God in your body and in your spirit, which are God's I should take care of my body, adorn my body, and use my body in a way that glorifies God.

1 Peter 4:16 Yet if anyone suffers as a Christian, let him not be ashamed, but let him glorify God in this matter.

Sometimes when we stand up for God and live the life He

wants us to live people we will be persecuted, and we will suffer. God tells us to use these moments to glorify Him. Jesus tells us how He glorified God.

John 17:4 I have glorified You on the earth. I have finished the work which You have given Me to do.

God has a plan for us and we are to be as diligent as Jesus was to do what God says to do and take advantage of the opportunities He gives us.

Matthew 25:31-40 "When the Son of Man comes in His glory, and all the holy angels with Him, then He will sit on the throne of His glory. All the nations will be gathered before Him, and He will separate them one from another, as a shepherd divides his sheep from the goats. And He will set the sheep on His right hand, but the goats on the left. Then the King will say to those on His right hand, 'Come, you blessed of My Father, inherit the kingdom prepared for you from the foundation of the world: for I was hungry and you gave Me food; I was thirsty and you gave Me drink; I was a stranger and you took Me in; I was naked and you clothed Me; I was sick and you visited Me; I was in prison and you came to Me.' "Then the righteous will answer Him, saying, 'Lord, when did we see You hungry and feed You, or thirsty and give You drink, When did we see You a stranger and take You in, or naked and clothe You? Or when did we see You sick, or in prison, and come to you? And the King will answer and say to them, 'Assuredly, I say to you, since you did it to one of the least of these My brethren, you did it to Me."

These are the opportunities we must glorify God through our simple actions.

1 John 3:16 By this we know love, because He laid down His life for us. And we also ought to lay down our lives for the brethren.

REFLECTION

As we prepared to leave for our fourth trip to Malawi we were going with sorrow in our hearts. The struggles that Malawi has seen throughout the past year have been daunting. A cyclone that doubled back and destroyed roads, homes, and crops has led to refugee camps where people must sneak away to worship God.

The Cholera Epidemic has been exasperated by the contaminated water and threatens thousands of lives. Malaria, a mosquito-borne disease, is spreading because of the stagnant waters left by the storms, and criminals have distributed malaria medicine that is nothing of the sort. That was accentuated when a ferry closing the Seri River was turned over by a hippopotamus and many were killed by the crocodiles and other hippos. They may be vegetarians, but they are some of the most dangerous animals in the world.

Recently our friend, brother, and interpreter, Shad, sent us a video. It is a picture of two women crossing a dilapidated bridge over a river that has crocodiles carrying a load of goods and a baby on one of the woman's backs. At one point they are walking in sandals on a string. My first comment to my husband was, "You used to build bridges for the Army you need to build them a bridge." The village, deep within the country has no roads, or outlets that would allow for that to be done. That is when Shad taught me another lesson. You must not show or tell the women that things can be easier because now this is what they are used to so they do it. If they have it easier for a while they will not work when it is once again hard.

As much as we would like to do in Malawi, the Lord is continually reminding me of the lesson He taught Martha. There is always much to do but to choose to learn and teach God's word is that which is most important. Luke 10:42, Mary had chosen the better part and Jesus would not take that away from her.

CHAPTER 13

PRAYER
Pemphero

REFLECTION

Many of the prayers that we pray prior to our trips to Malawi, those prayed there, and all year around are for wisdom. Let us know what to pray, let God's will be done. That statement was severely tested in the summer of 2019, the year COVID hit, we had planned to make our second trip to Malawi that year when the travel bans were put in place. Thinking I knew best and that we should go no matter what it took I frantically started scheming. We could go through South Africa, that route was closed. We could go through Mozambique, that route was closed. Finally, we were going to try to go through Zambia, and take a bus to the Malawi border where a king of a village had agreed to get us across. That was illegal and my husband, Larry, and Shad were brave enough to tell me that the trip would have to be canceled. I fell to the floor weeping not understanding how this could be God's will. The next day I was admitted to the hospital with a drug interaction that could have been fatal. After four days of inpatient care, I understood what God was trying to show me. He knows best, a prayer of a righteous person avails much, but God loves us too much and knows too much to lead us into circumstances that will harm us if we listen to how He answers our prayers. *James 5:16, Jeremiah 29:11, and Romans 8:28.*

When we did return, teaching supplies were limited to what we brought. This made for exciting innovations. One morning, we woke to the women and children wanting to learn. We had not planned for this so there was no paper and the only pens we had were our personal pens. But we did have a linen laundry bag and gel pens. This is a picture of them learning the books of the Bible and our "whiteboard" was much more important than the average laundry bag.

In our lives we learn early who to ask for specific things. A child knows to go to a mother for milk. Just like this there are things we need to go to God for. The first is wisdom.

James 1:5 If any of you lacks wisdom, let him ask of God, who gives to all liberally and without reproach, and it will be given to him.

Wisdom is the tool that we use to apply knowledge. When I was at a village and I wanted to help wash the dishes, I went over and watched how the sister wet her hand, patted it in the mud, and then used her hand to scrub the pot. I then mimicked her actions to clean a pot. Others soon came over and told me to use a wrap while I was working. I refused, it seemed so pretty, and I did not want to get their wrap dirty. They quickly settled the argument when they wrapped it around me before I knew what they were doing. They knew it was important that I have the protection of the wrap, which was wisdom. And that comes from God.

Romans 15:13 Now may the God of hope fill you with all joy and peace in believing, that you may abound in hope by the power of the Holy Spirit.

We need to pray for hope, that God will fill us with the joy and peace that comes from doing His will.

Psalm 119:18 Open my eyes, that I may see wondrous things from Your law.

We need to ask God to give us access to His word, and for the understanding so that we can see how powerful and what a blessing God's word is to us.

1 Thessalonians 5:16-18 Rejoice always, pray without ceasing, in everything give thanks; for this is the will of God in Christ Jesus for you.

Prayer is not supposed to be like a child who says "give me this and give me that" all the time. We are to give thanks to God for all the ways He blesses us.

Colossians 4:2-4 Continue earnestly in prayer, being vigilant in it with thanksgiving; meanwhile praying also for us, that God would open to us a door for the word to speak the mystery of Christ, for which I am also in chains, that I make it manifest, as I ought to speak.

As we pray thanking God for what He gives us we also need to pray that He will help those who are taking His word to others.

Luke 18:1-5 He spoke a parable to them, that men always ought to pray and not lose heart, saying: "There was in a certain city a judge who did not fear God nor regard man. Now there was a widow in that city; and she came to him, saying, 'Get justice for me from my adversary.' And he would not for a while; but afterward, he said within himself, 'Though I do not fear God nor regard man, yet because this widow troubles me I will avenge her, lest by her continual coming she weary me.'

Jesus teaches us here that there is a benefit to keep on asking.

Psalm 55:17 Evening and morning and at noon I will pray, and cry aloud, And He shall hear my voice.

God answers prayers, and sometimes, He is just waiting to hear us ask.

CHAPTER 14

KEEP GOD'S PERSPECTIVE
Knalani ndi Chiyembekezo cha Mulungu

Sometimes we get ahead of ourselves and think that we are in control.

Isaiah 10:15 Shall the ax boast itself against him who chops with it?

God knows where we can be used best and has given us the skills that we need to fulfill His plans. When we question that, look at things through our perspective rather than God's, we have the wrong perspective.

2 Corinthians 3:4-5 And we have such trust through Christ toward God.

When we decide to divert God's plans to go the way that we think is best instead of what He thinks we will not succeed. But, when we decide to just trust and do what God says He guarantees our success.

1 Corinthians 15:10 But by the grace of God I am what I am, and His grace toward me was not in vain; but I labored more abundantly than they all, yet not I, but the grace of God which was with me.

God has given us so many talents, opportunities, and blessings that we should work all the harder to accomplish his plans and share His love with others.

2 Corinthians 12:9-10 And He said to me, "My grace is sufficient for you for My strength is made perfect in weakness. Therefore most gladly I will rather boast in my infirmities, that the power of Christ may rest upon me. Therefore I take pleasure in infirmities, in reproaches, in needs. In persecution, in distress, for Christ's sake. For when I am weak, then I am strong.

We need to be willing to be anything to let God shine, even if we see that as demeaning. God was willing to send His Son, to die on a cross to save us and others. What are we willing to do to share His message with others?

2 Timothy 2:1 You, therefore, my son, be strong in the grace that is in Christ Jesus.

REFLECTION

Lazarus is one of the most encouraging individuals we work with in Malawi. He was the first person to interpret for me and had his work cut out. Doing so meant he would have to attend the women's classes instead of the men's, a very demeaning thing to ask of a Malawi man. He was also asked to help interpret children's songs, like This Little Light of Mine to Chichewa; that is a task easier said than done. He also establishes communication with the different village congregations. He sets up our very fluid schedule, an unenviable task because there is no way we can go to all who request we come.

One morning, at 5 am, he was riding his motorcycle, carrying his wife and son, all of whom were a part of the day's itinerary. Then the unthinkable occurred; they were hit by a car that tried to flee the scene. God was with them, the wife and son only had scratches, but Lazarus was not as fortunate. He had numerous injuries, including a broken leg that threatened to leave him lame. Three surgeries were required over a year to enable him to walk again without aid. But that did not stop him. He still planned for meetings, attended, and spoke. His encouragement and courage were true examples for us all.

CHAPTER 15

ENCOURAGEMENT
Chilimbikitso

This world is often full of disappointment, but we have hope in Christ and His words.

Romans 15:4 For whatever things were written before were written for our learning, that we through the patience and comfort of the Scriptures might have hope.

God gives us encouragement to help build our endurance for this life.

Hebrews 10:36 For you have need of endurance, so that after you have done the will of God, you may receive the promise. God reminds us throughout scripture that we have hope in Him.

Lamentations 3:21-24 This I recall to my mind, Therefore I have hope. Through the Lord's mercies, we are not consumed, Because His compassions fail not. They are new every morning; Great is Your faithfulness. The Lord is my portion, says my soul, Therefore I hope in Him.

The only reason we have any hope in this life and the one to come is because of God's mercies.

Proverbs 18:10 The name of the Lord is a strong tower; The righteous run to it and are safe.

We need to remember that whenever our burdens start to weigh us down we need to run to Him for help. Sometimes we feel like we need to come up with the strength to make it through our trials. But that is not the case. God provides our strength if we will just wait on Him.

Isaiah 40:31 But those who wait on the Lord Shall renew their strength; They shall mount up with wings like eagles, they shall run and not be weary. They shall walk and not faint.

We need to remind ourselves that God is there for us no matter what our trials are.

Psalms 23:4 Yea, though I walk through the valley of the shadow of death, I will fear no evil; for You are with me; Your rod and Your staff, they comfort me.

When we do this, and trust God with our problems the world will notice our faith and ask what assurance we have.

Deuteronomy 31:6 Be strong and of good courage, do not fear nor be afraid of them; for the Lord your God, He is the One who goes with you. He will not leave you nor forsake you.

Sometimes we are tempted to think that we know best and question God's plans but that is when we get in trouble.

Jeremiah 29:11 For I know the thoughts that I think toward you, says the Lord, thoughts of peace and not of evil, to give you a future and a hope.

So God's admonition for us is in our last verse.

Joshua 1:9 Have I not commanded you? Be strong and of good courage; do not be afraid, nor be dismayed, for the Lord goest where ever thou goes.

REFLECTION

In all of this I have learned that God has a plan even when we do not and if rejoicing with sisters across the globe is a foretaste of heaven, then we are truly in for something special. *Ndimakukondani alongo anga*! I love you my sisters!

ABOUT THE AUTHOR

Misti Stevens is a loving wife, mother, grandmother, and devoted servant of God because of His great love, blessings, and call. She has taught for 30 years in a wide variety of schools, states, and countries. She is currently an Adjunct Professor at Grand Canyon University and Florida College where she instructs Teacher Candidates and teaches American History. Her passion is to take God to those the world considers the "least of these" but are often the richest in faith and bloom when empowered through knowledge and compassion.